Preface

You may be a school library media specialist who works in a school library media center or a teacher-librarian who works in a high school library or a librarian who works in an elementary setting. With so many different labels within one profession, how do we speak in one voice to let the public know who we are and the crucial role we all play in impacting the bottom line—student achievement?

The answer is in your hands.

The American Library Association (ALA) in partnership with the American Association of School Librarians (AASL) has developed a national campaign to support school library media specialists in delivering a strong and clear message. This campaign addresses several key issues. These include how to:

- Increase awareness of and support for the role of school library media programs;
- Build understanding and appreciation for the value of school librarians;

- Help school librarians to market their programs;
- Position school librarianship as a dynamic career opportunity.

Tough economic times and advances in technology have raised questions about the role and value of school library media programs. In this toolkit, you will find marketing, branding and other communication strategies to support you in addressing these and other concerns.

By speaking out—and reaching out—with shared messages and strategies, you will help to build visibility and support for school library media programs and professionals nationwide.

To download the new print-ready graphics for school libraries, go to www.ala.org/@yourlibrary, click on *School Library Campaign*, and then *Graphics*.

Introduction

You are about to undertake an important process— marketing your program and yourselves as school library media specialists. This promotional process is based on the input we received from focus groups conducted by KRC Research, a market research company, for this campaign.

Two key findings:

- Parents and students feel that school library media programs are important only for younger children (elementary school age). *As students get older, computer use without a professional is perceived as the norm and professional guidance is not seen as necessary.*
- Many parents and students do not view library media specialists as educated professionals.

These findings underscore the need to change perceptions about who we are and what we do. The School Library Campaign is designed to help us do this by focusing on three key messages:

1) School library media programs are critical to the learning experience. School library media specialists collaborate with teachers and integrate literature and information skills into the curriculum to impact student achievement.

2) School library media specialists are crucial to the teaching and learning process. We teach skills and strategies that make a positive impact on student achievement and create lifelong learners.

3) School library media centers are places of opportunity where students can strive for and achieve success, develop a love of reading and explore the world around them through print, electronic and other media.

This *Toolkit* will help you to get these messages out to our many constituencies: students, teachers/administrators, parents, boards of education, legislators and our communities.

We wish you success in this endeavor. The promotional/marketing process will help to create a more positive image of our profession. It will also promote job retention and greater academic credibility among our colleagues and the wider school community.

Collegially,

Frances Roscello

Frances Roscello, President (2003–2004)
American Association of School Librarians

Harriet Selverstone

Harriet Selverstone, Chair (2002–2004)
AASL Special Committee for the @ your library® School Library Campaign

The Campaign for America's Libraries: Spotlight on School Libraries

The Campaign for America's Libraries is a multi-year public education campaign sponsored by ALA to speak loudly and clearly about the value of libraries and librarians in the 21st century. During 2003-2004, school library media programs and specialists are featured. The School Library Campaign was launched at the national conference of the American Association of School Librarians held October 22–26, 2003.

Goals

The new campaign, developed in collaboration with AASL, seeks to:

- Increase public awareness of the significant contributions made by school library media specialists through school library media programs to further the academic achievement and lifelong learning of our students;
- Strengthen a belief in the value of school library media programs and school library media specialists;
- Position school librarianship as a desirable career opportunity.

The Brand

What do McDonald's, Target and Starbucks have that libraries don't when it comes to their public image? They all have a brand so well known that all it takes is the glimpse of a golden arch, a target or a mermaid to achieve instant recognition.

ALA's Campaign for America's Libraries is our first attempt to achieve that same strong presence by providing a registered trademark—@ your library®—for use by all types of libraries across the nation. This brand is intended to give a distinct feel to our campaign, to break through the clutter of competing messages and establish a clear and unique identity.

The @ your library® logo, sample slogans and ready-to-print graphics for school library media programs can be downloaded at *www.ala.org/@yourlibrary*. Click on *School Library Campaign* and then *Graphics*. New slogans for

school library media programs include:

- Every student succeeds @ your library
- Get more out of class @ your library
- Got questions, get answers @ your library
- Make the grade @ your library
- Get connected @ your library
- Open a book, open your mind @ your library
- Get the score @ your library

You will want to review the trademark use policy and guidelines to help you reap the benefits of using the brand and maximize its impact nationwide. Also see **"Putting the @ your library® Brand to Work"** on page 5.

Audiences

Primary audiences for the campaign are teachers and administrators, students and parents, and boards of education. Secondary audiences are legislators and the community at large.

Key Messages

The campaign's key messages focus on the unique value and characteristics of school library media programs, centers and specialists. The messages were developed based on research (focus groups and interviews) conducted by KRC Research, a subsidiary of Weber Shandwick Worldwide, a public relations and communication management firm that has worked with ALA to design The Campaign for America's Libraries. For more about the research conducted, go to *www.ala.org/@yourlibrary*. Click on *School Library Campaign* and then *Research*.

Strategies

The campaign is designed to support school library media programs in reaching out to key audiences by:

- helping to unify and maximize the communications efforts of ALA, AASL and school library media programs nationwide;

- providing messages, tools and resources to promote their value;
- sharing "best practices" in library marketing and public relations.

Partners

Thanks to a partnership with the International Federation of Library Associations and Institutions (IFLA), a Campaign for the World's Libraries is reaching the international library community. To date, more than 20 countries have joined the world campaign by signing international trademark agreements. These include Armenia, Australia, Azerbaijan, Belarus, Brazil, Bulgaria, Canada, the Caribbean, Georgia, Iceland, Italy, Japan, Kazakhstan, Korea, Mexico, Moldova, Nepal, Nigeria, Portugal, Serbia, Singapore, Turkey, and Venezuela. The @ your library® logo is being translated into all of these countries' respective languages. Artwork, informational materials and a consumer-oriented video have been translated into Spanish, as well.

Founding partners of The Campaign for America's Libraries include 3M Library Systems, the Center for the Book in the Library of Congress, the International Federation of Library Associations and Institutions (IFLA), Major League Baseball, Morningstar Foods Inc. (maker of Hershey®'s Milk), the National Aeronautics and Space Administration (NASA), Wells Fargo Home Mortgage and *Woman's Day* magazine.

New Tools and Training

@ your library® Toolkit for School Library Media Programs

Use this toolkit to develop or enhance a marketing communication program for your school library and to build on the success of the American Library Association's (ALA) national Campaign for America's Libraries.

Talk About It

AASLPR, a new discussion list for school library media specialists, is an opportunity to share ideas and ask questions about promotion and marketing. To subscribe, send a message to *subscribe-aaslpr@ala.org* with your first and last name as the subject. Leave the body of the message blank.

Ready-to-Print Graphics

New graphics are available using the @ your library® brand to help you promote your library and the national ALA/AASL School Library Campaign. Templates, as well as other artwork, are available for use on ads, bookmarks, brochures, flyers and more at *www.ala.org/@yourlibrary* under *School Library Campaign.* Click on *Graphics.*

Sharpen Your Marketing Skills

3M Library Systems, a founding partner in the @ your library® campaign, and AASL have put together a package of materials to help school library media specialists prepare multi-year marketing plans using the @ your library® brand. Materials are in moduals and can be used to train others to lead discussions or can be used in your own library. The following materials are available:

- Strategic Marketing for School Library Media Centers Facilitator Guide
- Strategic Marketing for School Library Media Centers Facilitator Slides
- Strategic Marketing for School Library Media Centers Train the Trainer Slides
- Strategic Marketing for School Library Media Centers Participant Manual

If you are interested in becoming a trainer or sponsoring or attending a training session, please send e-mail to: *aasl@ala.org.* Training materials can be downloaded from the 3M Library Systems Web site at *www.3m.com/us/library.* For more helpful materials for promoting and advocating for school libraries, see "**More Tools**" on page 39.

Wanted: Your Good Ideas

We encourage you to to share how your library has used the @ your library® brand on our new database at *www.ala.org/@yourlibrary* under *Participating Libraries.* You can use the database to learn what other libraries have done. Search by state, type of library, outreach and/or communications effort. More than 47 outreach categories can be searched, including outreach to students and faculty, promotion of electronic resources, special events and School Library Media Month.

For More Information

Visit the campaign Web site at *www.ala.org/@yourlibrary*. Or contact the American Association of School Librarians. Tel: 800-545-2433 ext 1396 or *aasl@ala.org*.

Putting the @ your library® Brand to Work

Flexible and easy to adapt, the @your library® brand can be used to create your own slogans and artwork for programs and promotional materials such as newsletters, flyers, bookmarks, mouse pads and magnets. Brainstorm with school staff and students. Or, for more slogans, go to *www.ala.org/@yourlibrary*. Click on *School Library Campaign* and then *Marketing and Promotion*. See **"Who's on Board"** on page 6 for examples of how school library media centers have already used the brand.

Here are some ideas to get you started:

Students

Kindergarten-Elementary

- **It's a small world @ your library**—Use the theme for a series of multicultural displays and programming.
- **Read to your pet @ your library**—Ask kids to write about what they think their pet's favorite book would be and why. Have them take photos or draw pictures to accompany their piece. Display or post them in the library and on the Web site. Award prizes.
- **Get caught reading @ your library**—Take candid photos of children reading in the library and around school. Keep a running display in the library and on the Web page. Or, let children enter their name in a drawing for prizes every time they read a book.
- **Join the All-Stars @ your library**—Start your own All-Star Reading Team. Students must read a certain number of books. Work with a local sports team or business to get free or discounted seats at a sporting event for those who qualify. Or, invite members of a local team to visit your library and meet the Reading All-Stars.
- **Reading is fun @ your library**—Make or buy colorful bookmarks with lists of fun reading to give to children. Encourage them to write brief book reviews and put them in the front of books, in your newsletter and on the Web site.

Middle-High School

- **@ your library? @ your library!**—Sponsor an @ your library® slogan contest for students. Recruit school staff to serve as judges. Then take the winning slogans and use them.
- **Get the score @ your library**—Sponsor a series of clinics to coach students on preparing for tests, how to use databases, cite sources and other information literacy skills. Use a sports motif on promotional materials. (See the new "Get the Score" graphic available online.) Wear a sports cap and whistle around your neck when conducting a session.
- **Slammin' @ your library**—Plan a series of programs around poetry. Have students read a favorite poem—their own or someone else's—each day on the PA. Posters and a manual for creating a poetry slam are available from ALA Graphics.
- **Express yourself @ your library**—Sponsor workshops on various ways of expressing yourself. Invite authors, poets, artists, composers and musicians (of all types) to lead workshops. Feature the students' work via an art exhibit, talent show, special publication or Web site.
- **Come together @ your library**—Promote the library as a meeting place for classes and students, whether they're coming together for research, a class project or to work on homework with friends. Use the same slogan to reach out to teachers about how you can help them reach their classroom goals.

Teachers & Administrators

- **We're here for you @ your library**—Send a personalized welcome letter to invite faculty members to tour the media center and to let them know about special services/resources available to them and their students. Follow up with a call. (See "Sample Invitation" on page 14.)
- **Beyond the Web @ your library**—Offer training sessions for staff on how to create assignments that challenge students to go beyond the Web, how to use databases, surf the "invisible Web" and other 21st century research techniques.
- **Meet me @ your library**—Select a day, possibly an in-service day, and invite teachers for coffee and a

consultation on lesson plans or other needs they may have.

- **New! @ your library**—Send brief announcements about new books and a time when they will be available for review.
- **Happy reading @ your library**—Send a flyer wishing all staff a happy vacation along with a list of suggested reading.

Parents

- **One Book. One School @ your library**—Select a book for everyone—faculty and students—to read (or have teachers read to them). Send promotional materials to parents and encourage them to read and discuss the book with their children. Sponsor an author visit and/or book discussion at a time when parents can attend.
- **Parents connect @ your library**—Create and promote a special Parent's Page on your Web site with tips and resources to help parents help their children read, learn and use the Internet.
- **Every student succeeds @ your library**—Give presentations to the PTA or other parent and community groups about the important role school library media centers and specialists play in student achievement. Invite them to meet at the media center. Create a PowerPoint presentation using The Campaign for America's Libraries' template. Go to *www.ala.org* and click on *Issues and Advocacy* from the homepage. Then scroll down to *Resources* and click on *Conduct an Advocacy Presentation.*
- **Book some time @ your library**—Publish a simple but colorful flyer or brochure with tips for parents on how to encourage their child to read and use the library, how to use the Internet safely and the importance of encouraging children not to depend solely on the Internet for their homework needs.
- **Rally 'round @ your library**—Host a special meeting for parents to inform them of not just what you offer, but also of your media center's needs and how they can help, e.g., establishing a Friends of the Library group, raising money, volunteering their time.

Who's On Board

Here is a sampling of school library media centers and school library organizations that have already put the @

your library® brand to use. To learn more about how school library media centers are participating in the Campaign for America's Libraries, see *www.ala.org/ @yourlibrary*. Click on *Participating Libraries* to access the campaign's database and search under *School Library*.

North Elementary School

Noblesville, IN
The North Elementary School uses the theme "Untangle the Web @ your library" on its Web site at *www.nobl. k12.in.us/media/NorthMedia/index.htm*. The school's library media specialist introduced a program directed at teachers called "Find a partner @ your library." The library's monthly newsletter is titled "Media Matters @ your library."

Walled Lake Central High School

Walled Lake, MI
The library produced a commercial to promote National Library Week that used the slogan, "Research @ your library." The commercial was played during the school's video announcements to promote the library: "We don't give any grades or assignments. We make them better."

Curtis Senior High School

University Place, WA
The high school library promotes ethical use of research resources and respect for intellectual property rights with a banner that says, "Cite Your Sources @ your library." Examples of various types of resources students might need to cite are posted. Smaller signs with the slogan are taped to the top edge of each computer monitor as a reminder to students to be sure to collect bibliographic information as they are researching.

Park Hill School District

Kansas City, MO
Collaborating with Kansas City's Maple Woods Community College, selected schools in the Park Hill School District hosted storytellers as part of "Storytelling 2003 @ your library." A giant "@ your library" card was created. The card can be downloaded from the @ your library® Web site at *www.ala.org/@yourlibrary*. Click on *PR Tools and Resources.*

Reidland High School

Paducah, KY

Reidland High School posts an electronic newsletter on its Web site called "What's happening @ your library." Issues have featured events that are promoted with @ your library, such as "Lunch @ your library," an event that brought together members of the high school's class of 1940 and current students, and "Poetry contest @ your library," a contest to celebrate National Poetry Month. The library used "Check it out @ your library" to promote library happenings during 2003.

Lincoln Public Schools

Lincoln, NE

Among the first to get on board the @ your library® campaign, the Lincoln Public Schools (LPS) have integrated the @ your library® brand into a number of programs and promotions, from staff development ("Information Literacy @ your library") to a monthly communication flyer that goes out to teachers and administrators ("Principle Picks @ your library"). The @ your library brand has appeared on the Web site and on bookmarks for students, staff and administrators ("Online anytime @ your library"). The staff is working to develop an ongoing column in "Free Times," a newsletter that goes out to parents, using @ your library. Elementary schools have used the @ your library® logo with slogans such as "Read Across America @ your library," "Lowry @ your library" or "Search for answers @ your library."

New York State Education Department & the School Library Media Section of the New York Library Association

The New York State Education Department promotes its "School Library Media Program Improvement Initiative" with the slogan "Information Literacy @ your library."

The slogan has been printed on pins and lanyards. The pins were also used at the 2002 conference of the School Library Media Section of the New York Library Association, which had the theme "Information Literacy @ your library." The 2003 theme was "Celebrate Success @ your library."

Tucson Unified School District

Tucson, AZ

@ your library was incorporated into a brochure to help district principals evaluate their school's teacher librarians and learn about what they do. It includes "everything you need to know about evaluating your professional teacher-librarian but were afraid to ask" and promotes teacher-librarians as "a critical component in 21st century education."

Anacortes High School

Anacortes, WA

"What's really happening . . . @ your library" was the theme of a PowerPoint presentation and notebook intended to raise awareness among district administrators about what school librarians do. Each principal in the district as well as the superintendent received copies of the notebook. @ your library is also featured on the high school's Web page at *http://ahs. asd103.org/Library/@yourlibrary.htm,* along with the PowerPoint presentation.

Moscow Elementary Schools

Moscow, ID

Every month the Moscow Elementary librarian makes at least one bookmark that uses the @ your library® logo. The bookmarks are distributed to the area's four elementary libraries. Slogans have included "You're 1st @ your library" and "Get big with books @ your library."

Speaking Out

If we don't speak out, who will? The School Library Campaign provides an opportunity for library media specialists to make our voice heard in schools and communities across America. AASL members developed the core messages for the School Library Campaign based on research that found:

- Middle and high school students and their parents place a lower value on the library media program than do elementary students and parents.
- Principals and teachers are most likely to see the value in schoool libraries and librarians—for students. They tend to turn elsewhere for their own needs.
- Many parents and students do not see librarians as educated professionals who play an active role in the academic community.
- Library media specialists and media centers are perceived as more positive and professional terms—but only when the library is equipped with computers and other technology.

For more about the research conducted, go to *www.ala. org/aasl*. Look under *Professional Tools* for *@ your library®️ Campaign for School Libraries,* or visit the *School Library Campaign* section of the *@ your library®️* Web site and click on *Research*.

Key Messages

The core messages for the campaign are:

School library media programs are critical to the learning experience.
- School library media programs, where school library media specialists collaborate with classroom teachers to teach and integrate literature and information skills into the curriculum, make a positive impact on student achievement.
- School library media specialists work with classroom teachers on cooperative and collaborative projects to help students use a variety of resources, conduct research and present their findings.
- School library media programs are integral to achieving the mission of the school and are supported fiscally and programmatically by the educational community.

- School library media programs are integrated within the school technology plan and are integral to all teaching and learning.

School library media specialists are crucial to the teaching and learning process.
- School library media specialists teach skills and strategies students need to learn and achieve.
- School library media specialists are partners in educating students, developing curricula and integrating resources into teaching and learning.
- School library media specialists teach students skills they need to become effective users of ideas and information.
- School library media specialists seek, select, evaluate and utilize electronic resources and tools and instruct teachers and students in how to use them.

School library media centers are places of opportunity.
- SLMCs are places where all students can strive for and achieve success.
- SLMCs are places that provide quality collections in print and online that support the curriculum and address a variety of learning needs.
- SLMCs are places to develop a love of reading and literature.
- SLMCs are places where school library media specialists help students explore the world around them through print and electronic media.
- SLMCs are places where students can work individually or in small groups on research and collaborative projects and share their learning.

Sample Message Sheet

Having a consistent message is key to a successful awareness campaign. Think about what messages you remember, and chances are they are the ones that have been around the longest. Having a one-page message sheet with your key message and three talking points adapted for key audiences can help keep you and your advocates "on message." You will want to use these messages as often and consistently as possible in presentations, print, electronic and other communications. You are encouraged to adapt this sample message sheet for your library media program and to add stories and examples that illustrate key points. Try to speak in language and give examples that resonate with your various audiences. Avoid technical language or professional jargon that may not be easily understood.

Telling Our Story

- Once upon a time there was a 5th grader who didn't like to read. In fact, he rarely read for pleasure and he never set foot in our media center unless forced to. Today, he is an avid reader, and his reading and math levels have both gone up a notch. Why? Because Sam, like just about every other kid in our school, loves our remodeled media center. He loves the bright colors, the big pillows to sit on and the computers. But most of all, he loves our bigger and better collection of books.
- Karen, a 9th grader, was on the verge of failing social studies after being caught repeatedly plagiarizing from Web sites. Today, she aces her research assignments with projects that don't rely solely on the Internet and respect intellectual property rights. Karen credits her new skills to the library media specialist and the media center's information literacy program.

Success stories, like the ones above, bring our message to life in a way that numbers alone can't. Although you will want to make strategic use of statistics, numbers aren't the whole story when it comes to telling our story.

Why? Because everyone loves a story, especially one with a happy ending. Also, most people don't remember statistics unless they are surprisingly good or bad or translated into stories, e.g., "Americans spend more money on snack food than school libraries." And while a few statistics can help make your story, a few too many can kill it.

Whether it's a presentation to the school board, a brochure for parents or casual conversation with a teacher, you should be prepared with at least three stories or examples to illustrate how your library media program makes a difference.

Tough Questions

In making yourself more visible, you may also be confronted with more challenging questions on sensitive

Sample Message Sheet

Key Message
Every student succeeds at your school library.

Talking Points
Students
- The library is one place where you're *not* expected to have the answers. We're here to teach you how to find them.
- You may think you're wired. But unless you're connected to your school library you don't know what you're missing.
- Everything you want to know about practically everything is at your school library. And the library media specialist is there to help you find it.

Teachers/Administrators
- We're here for you at the (name) library. Our mission is to help every student develop a love of reading, become a skilled user of ideas and information and explore the world through print and electronic media.
- School library media specialists teach information skills and strategies that students need to learn and achieve.
- The school library media center provides print, electronic and other resources that support the curriculum and address a variety of learning needs.

Parents
- Our school library is more than books. It is a learning hub with a full range of print and electronic media that support student achievement.
- School library media specialists teach information skills that students need to learn and achieve for a lifetime.
- Research shows a direct link between student achievement and school library media programs stocked with a full range of resources and staffed by library media specialists.

School Boards/Legislators
- There is no such thing as good education without good school libraries.
- School library media programs contribute directly to the bottom line—student achievement.
- Research shows there is a direct link between student achievement and library media programs stocked with a full range of resources and staffed by library media specialists.

topics. Every library has its own "tough" questions. Anticipate them and prepare answers. Knowing the answers will help you to feel—and appear—more confident, as well as give better answers. In responding to questions, remember that these are opportunities to deliver your key message. Also keep in mind the following:

- Keep your answer *positive.* Never repeat negative language.
- Don't "overtalk" your answers. Giving too much information may only provoke more challenging questions.
- It's not just what you say but how you say it. Speak simply, sincerely and with conviction.

The sample questions and answers below are intended as a guide. ALA's *Library Advocate's Handbook* provides more information about dealing with tough questions (see **"More Tools"** on page 39).

1. Isn't everything available on the Internet? Why do we need a school library?

Our school library is more than books. It's a learning hub with a full range of print and electronic resources that support student achievement. These resources include books, magazines, videotapes, computers, databases and much more. More importantly, there is a school library media specialist to assist students with their information needs and help teachers develop projects that engage students in developing critical learning and research skills.

2. Why do we need a school library media specialist? Can't we use volunteers?

School library media specialists have advanced education degrees as teachers and librarians. They understand how to teach and are experts in children's and young adult literature, as well as information science. They know what kids like to read and what is appropriate at different stages of their development. They understand how information is organized and how to find it in many different formats—print and electronic. They are there to help classroom teachers teach and students to learn using a variety of resources. Few volunteers have the expertise to do this.

How do you collect stories?

1. Encourage students and teachers to share their school library success stories. Award prizes. Post them on the Web site and feature them in your newsletter. Possibly in connection with Library Lovers Month in February or School Library Media Month in April. (See "Calendar of Promotional Opportunities", pg. 36.)
2. Work with a journalism teacher to have students conduct interviews and report on how the school library media program makes a difference.
3. Send a note of congratulations to seniors with a brief survey asking them to share what they liked best about the school library media center, how it helped them and any suggestions they might have, especially for incoming students. Create a display featuring some of the better responses with photos.
4. Save and quote from thank-you notes sent by teachers, students or parents.

Stories often can be used without names. When using students' names or pictures, be sure to follow your school's policies. For examples of quotes from students, see those collected by the Baltimore County Public Schools before and after a school library remodeling project at *www.bcpl.net/ ~dcurtis/libraryfacts/kids.html.*

Share your best stories with the @ your library® School Library Campaign by sending them to *aasl@ala.org.*

---

3. Isn't it true students don't use the library anymore?

On the contrary! Our library is filled with students throughout the day . . . reading books, logging on to the Internet, getting help with research projects, studying, working on projects with other students and lots more. Not only that, our Web site is used by students for homework and other research after school. I encourage you to visit our library and Web site and see for yourself.

4. Why would I want to be a school librarian?

Being a school library media specialist is extremely rewarding. The salary is the same as classroom teachers and continues to rise. But the real pay off is the satisfaction you get from helping students discover the joy of reading and learn essential information literacy skills. I feel like I'm making a difference in their lives not just today, but 10 or 20 years from now. As a profession, librarians are committed to protecting the freedom to read and ensuring that information is freely available to all. I'm proud to be part of that.

5. Why should the library get more money when we have to cut other areas?

There is no such thing as good education without a good library. Studies have shown there is a direct link between student achievement and library media centers that are professionally staffed and well stocked with books and technology (see **"More Tools/Research"** on page 39). In the last five years, our media center's buying power has decreased by *[add number here]* percent. Without an increase, we cannot provide the quality or quantity of resources that our students and teaching staff deserve.

6. Since everything is electronic, shouldn't the library need less money?

Technology offers many advantages, but saving money isn't necessarily one of them. Computers and other electronic resources must be maintained, updated and staffed. Also, everything is far from electronic. Our library has a large collection of books, magazines, videos and other learning resources that aren't on the Internet—and probably never will be. Our students must be skilled in using many different media if they are to succeed in today's world.

7. What is "information literacy" anyway?

Information literacy means knowing how to find, evaluate and use information from a variety of sources. It means knowing when a book may be more helpful than a Web site. It means knowing what questions to ask. Is the information complete? Accurate? Is someone trying to sell something? Good decisions depend on good information. School library media specialists know that the best source of information isn't always Google. They teach 21st century research skills that students will use throughout their lives.

8. Why should we invest in books when they have the Internet?

Our students need both if they are to learn and achieve. If students are to learn how to be effective consumers of information, they must understand and be able to use many different media. The Internet, for instance, is useful primarily for current information. Books and other print resources offer a greater breadth and depth of information than can be found online. Sometimes a video is a better learning tool than a book or the Internet.

Get more out of class

@ your library®

School library media programs are key to student achievement and lifelong learning.

The Campaign for America's Libraries

To download the new print-ready graphics for school libraries, go to *www.ala.org/@yourlibrary,* click on *School Library Campaign,* and then *Graphics.*

Reaching Out

Marketing your library means making a conscious, proactive effort to reach out and show that the media center is a changing and dynamic place and that you bring special expertise. It means staying visible and keeping in touch. It means reaching out with special programs that focus attention on what you offer and promoting a sense of ownership.

Developing a reputation as someone who not only delivers but delights is one of the best and fastest ways to turn those you work with into your advocates. One school library media specialist makes a special effort to visit every teacher at least once during the school year to discuss his/her curriculum needs. She sweetens these meetings by bringing a homemade cookie.

Whenever possible, try to bust the stereotypes with programs and activities that let students, teachers, administrators and parents know the library is a welcoming, "with it" place staffed by people who understand and care about their needs.

Students

- Form a student advisory group to advise and assist in developing programming and promotions directed at students. Consider them part of your marketing team.
- Take part in major activities such as homecoming or prom. Provide etiquette tips. Help decorate the gym. One high school library in North Carolina offers a prom fashion show with students as models.
- Listen—don't just talk. Put out a "Talk Back" suggestion box inviting students to ask questions or share what they like and don't like about the library. Post frequently asked questions and the answers.
- Put "tent cards" (similar to those often found on restaurant tables) featuring the library's Web site/other services in the cafeteria/lunch room.
- Sponsor contests on- and offline that challenge students' research skills and entice them to log on/visit the media center.
- Invite students and staff to display their collections and/or hobbies, as well as school projects.
- Ask faculty to include a library message, e.g., "Got questions? Get answers! @ your library," on class handouts.

- Hang colorful @ your library® banners outside the library, in hallways, eating areas and the gym.
- Contribute articles on a regular basis to the student newspaper. Make a point of letting students and their parents know about grants, awards, scholarships and other opportunities.
- Build the buzz. If you know a student is pleased with the assistance you provided, ask her/him to spread the word.

Faculty & Administrators

- Make it clear that you are there to help achieve the school's mission. Create a mission statement for the media program aligned with the school's mission and display it proudly—and prominently—in the media center, on your Web site and in publications.
- Invite their participation. One school library sponsors a fairy tale festival where the principal and teachers dress as storybook characters. Many principals have kissed pigs, shaved their heads and sat on roofs in the cause of reading.
- Get 'em while they're new. Send a welcome package at the beginning of the school year with a library brochure and other materials to new staff, students and parents. Request to be a part of the new teacher induction seminars if your district provides them.
- Share success stories—in staff meetings, publications, on the Web site, whenever and wherever possible. Keep them brief.
- Give them their own space. Provide a professional reading corner or space to exchange their previously read books and magazines.
- Volunteer to serve on a variety of committees. Insert the library media program into all schoolwide activities.
- Collect and report examples of how teachers and students have developed projects or curricula in collaboration with the media specialist. Create displays and feature them in your newsletter. Nominate them for awards.
- Aim to communicate on a regular basis. Provide copies of your newsletter, annual report, promotional flyers and other items of special interest. Use email but don't rely on it. Ask how often and what format (print or email) they prefer to receive updates.

- Develop a reputation for fun, as well as hard work. Look for excuses to invite staff to the media center for fun and treats, whether it's School Library Media Month, Teacher's Appreciation Week, the Academy Awards or A.A. Milne's birthday. (See **"Calendar of Promotional Opportunities"** on page 35.)
- Use food as bait. If you add a new database or feature to your Web site, offer demonstrations with the additional enticement of coffee and doughnuts or pizza. Ask the Friends of the Library or local businesses to underwrite refreshments and recognize them in school newsletters.
- Start your own brag board with thank you notes and favorable comments from staff, students and parents. Also feature them on your Web site and in the newsletter.
- Send personal notes on Post-it® pads or note pads with your favorite quotes about libraries and librarians such as "Librarians rule!" (Regis Philbin.) (To order customized pads, see *www.3M.com.*)

Parents & Caregivers

- Make sure an "Every student succeeds @ your library" welcome message from the media specialist appears in back-to-school packets for parents.
- Write a regular column in the school newsletter for parents. Include mini-reviews of books, Web sites and other helpful resources.
- Create and promote a special Parent's Page on your Web site with tips and resources to help parents help their children read, learn and use the media center, as well as the Internet.
- Host special tours/reception for parents during parent-teacher night or School Library Media Month. Focus on the resources, especially online, that weren't around when they were in school.
- Offer classes and workshops on topics like Beyond the Web: What you should know to help your child or How to Raise a Reader.
- Work with teachers and school counselors to identify children whose parents have language or reading difficulties. Provide a list of community resources that can help them.
- Offer a special collection on parenting and education for parents.
- Sponsor regular family nights with storytelling, films and other activities.
- Invite parents to participate in special programs on

careers, cultural diversity, writing and the arts.
- Start a Friends of the Library group to assist with fundraising and other special projects. (See **"Forming a Friends Group"** on page 25.)

Community

- Start a reader's theatre for students. Schedule performances at senior centers, public libraries and other venues.
- Make presentations to business and service groups about the changing role of today's school library media center.
- Ask a service group to adopt your media center as a fundraising project or to provide volunteer assistance.
- Invite local journalists to participate in discussions of the First Amendment.
- Invite seniors and others to serve as reading tutors and homework helpers.
- Ask the local book editor or newspaper editor to run a special section of student book reviews during Teen Read Week or Children's Book Week. (Coordinate with other media centers in the paper's circulation area.) For more suggestions, see **"Media Relations"** on page 20.
- Work with your public library to get 100 percent library card sign-up at your school. Ask local businesses to provide treats for the first class(s) to sign up.
- Invite local authors to conduct writing workshops for students or talk with them over lunch.
- Work with other libraries—school, public, academic and special—to develop broad-based programs such as the popular "One Book. One Community." (See **"Collaboration"** on page 16.)
- Contact community relations/education staff of museums to develop displays, projects and programming in connection with special exhibits they are hosting.

Sample Invitation

Print the letter on the following page on colorful paper with "Every student succeeds @ your library®" (graphic available online). Edit and add information as appropriate for staff or parents. If possible, follow up with calls to schedule visits.

Dear _____:

The beginning of a school year is filled with anticipation, and yes, hard work. To help support you and your students at this busy time, it is my pleasure to invite you to visit our School Library Media Center. Why?

Because we want you to know we're here for you and are eager to share what we can do for you and your students. We also want to learn more about your needs.

Our library media center is a gathering place for people, ideas, debate and exploration. Our mission is to help every student develop a love of reading, to become a skilled user of ideas and information and to explore the world through print and electronic media. We are pleased to assist with your curricular needs and welcome your suggestions for how we can better support you and your students.

Please join me for a personal tour of our resources—on- and offline. It will be well worth your time—no more than half an hour—and there'll be treats. Just let me know what would be a convenient time for you. You can reach me at *[extension and e-mail]*.

My best wishes for the coming school year. I look forward to welcoming you to our media center.

Sincerely,
[name], Library Media Specialist

Every student succeeds® @ your library®

School library media centers are places of opportunity.

The Campaign for America's Libraries

To download the new print-ready graphics for school libraries, go to *www.ala.org/@yourlibrary,* click on *School Library Campaign,* and then *Graphics.*

Marketing and Communication

In marketing, communicating about the service you provide is as important as delivering it. Listening is as important as telling, and consumer "wants" are as important as needs. Key steps in developing an overall marketing plan are:

- Research (to identify users/potential users, their needs and wants)
- Strategic planning (to develop a vision, goals, products, services)
- Communication (to promote what you offer)
- Evaluation (to strive for continual improvement)

In this toolkit, you will find messages, ideas and strategies to help you in developing a communication/promotion plan for your library media program. To learn more about creating an overall marketing plan, including planning worksheets, see *Every Student Succeeds @ your library: Strategic Marketing for School Library Media Centers* at *www.3M.com/us/library*.

Building a Communication Plan

The communication/marketing plan is an essential step in getting the word out about your school library media program. This plan should support the overall mission and goals of your library media program. It should be reviewed and updated annually, along with your marketing plan. Above all, it should be practical and doable. Use the outline below as a guide in developing your own marketing communication plan.

Introduction: What is the context of the communication activity?

Briefly outline problems and opportunities to be addressed, relevant data, other background. For example:
The school library media program and its staff are essential to the learning process but are not always recognized in school communications and planning functions.

Goals: What do you want to happen?

Describe the desired outcomes—your dream. Your communication goals should support your media center's overall goals. For example:
All teachers/administrators, students and parents will value the school library media program. They will be aware of and use the services available to them.

Objectives: What will be accomplished?

Objectives are doable and measureable. For example:
- *Strengthen the image and visibility of the school library media program by using the @ your library® brand.*
- *There will be a 15 percent increase in use by teachers.*
- *Circulation of materials will increase by 10 percent.*
- *The library will have a Friends group.*

- *The school community will join in celebrating School Library Media Month.*

Positioning statement: How do you want the library to be perceived?

Define the image you would like for your library. Consider the competition. What do you offer they don't? For example:
The school library media program provides critical resources and expertise to teachers and students in a comfortable, welcoming atmosphere. Our staff is friendly, knowledgeable and helpful. We promote a love of reading and teach information and research skills that students will use throughout their lives. We support all teachers and staff in achieving our school's mission.

Target audiences: Who needs to hear the message?

Your plan should prioritize your key audiences. This does not mean you will focus only on some and ignore others. It means that you will focus your time and resources where they are most needed. Some target audiences may change from year to year, while others will remain the same. You may also want to break down each audience by grade and other

(cont. on pg. 16)

Collaboration

Collaboration is a key strategy for making information power a reality and for increasing the visibility of the school library media program. It can take many forms . . . everything from fashion shows to oral history projects. In addition to teachers, it can involve other librarians, parents, community businesses and service groups—anyone who wants to help students succeed.

Three good examples from Pennsylvania:

- Eight public and 10 school libraries held a fashion show during Teen Read Week with middle and high school students modeling the latest fashions—and their favorite books. School librarians helped select models to represent their school. Local television and radio personalities emceed. A local mall provided free space and retailers provided fashions, hair styling and make up. The Blair County Library System provided $400 to cover pizza, ALA Celebrity Read Posters, Teen Read bookmarks and other giveaways. (Contact: Vivian Van Dyke, vvandyke@ altoonasd.com)

- Inspired by the Library of Congress' American Memory Project, 4th and 5th graders prepared PowerPoint presentations about family members' memories such as immigration to the U.S., a family heirloom, historic event or childhood recollection. The project involves library, technology and teaching staff from the Wickersham Elementary School, Lancaster Country Day School, Lancaster County Library, Library System of Lancaster County and Millersville University; also the Lancaster Literacy Guild. (Contact: Linda Carvell, carvelll@e-lcds.org)

- Students and seniors connect in a project sponsored by the media center of the Western Wayne Middle School and the Salem Public Library. Students send email to the public library's senior citizens group telling about their favorite objects and hobbies. Seniors respond by sharing the things they

---

categories you feel are useful.

Internal audiences include:
   Staff—full- and part-time
   Student assistants
   Volunteers
   Friends of the library
   Other?
External audiences include:
   Teachers
   Administrators
   Students
   Parents
   Board of education members
   Funders: Donors/Legislators/Taxpayers
   Prospective partners
   Media
   Other?

Key message(s): *What is the most important message you wish to deliver?*

Use your key message as often and as consistently as possible for maximum impact, e.g.:
Every student succeeds @ your library.

Strategies: *How will you deliver the message?*

Identify publicity and outreach activities aimed at your target audiences. You will need to identify a timetable and person responsible for each activity. Strategies for delivering the message include:

Banners/Posters/Displays
Handouts/Giveaways, e.g., bookmarks, mugs
Media: School and community newspapers, radio and TV
Print materials: annual report, newsletter, flyers, tent cards, etc.
Web sites
E-mail lists
Presentations to groups
Collaboration with other departments/organizations
Word of mouth

Evaluation measures: *How will you know what worked and what didn't?*

Your objectives should provide a clear means of evaluation. Frequently used measures include: circulation, Web site visits, attendance at programs, number of media stories placed/speeches given, follow-up surveys/interviews, word-of-mouth feedback, letters of appreciation, honors received. Review each strategy and why it did or didn't work. Use what you learned in making next year's communication plan.

cherished when they were that age. The discussion continues as each generation explains what has caused the changes in their lives, especially in regards to entertainment and social life. A PowerPoint presentation of the experience will be the culminating event when both groups come together to meet and talk face to face. (Contact: Michele Petrosky, *chlesfaeriedust@aol.com*)

Good communication is key to successful collaboration

Some tips:

- Use collaboration as an opportunity to educate about what you do. Don't assume that others (including other librarians) know what you have to offer.
- Do your homework. Don't assume you know what others have to offer. Be aware of any laws, school district or other policies that may apply.
- Be patient and persistent. Scheduling and details can be challenging when working with many parties.
- Make sure your principal and teaching staff are aware of the nature of the collaboration and the reasons behind it. Invite their input. Provide updates.
- Get to know the people you are working with. Invite them for coffee or lunch.
- Confirm goals and expectations in writing for all contributors.
- Make certain that everyone receives regular updates and has input in the publicity and reporting for the project.
- Build in an evaluation process.
- Be sure to thank everyone involved. Provide a summary of what was accomplished.

Contributors: M. Veanna Baxter, adjunct professor, Library Science and Information Technologies, Mansfield University, Mansfield, PA; principal of VBEC Library Consulting Services. A school librarian for 30 years, Baxter is immediate past president of the Pennsylvania School Librarians Association (PSLA). Susan Gilbert Beck, president of Emanda, Inc. and a consultant on access. For more information, see:

> ***The School Buddy System: The Practice of Collaboration**, Gail Bush. Chicago: American Library Association, 2002.*
> ***Collaboration: Lessons Learned**, Robert Grover, ed., American Association of School Librarians, 1996. To order call 866-SHOP ALA (866-746-7252).*

Working with School District PR Staff

Many school districts (and some schools) employ communications/public relations professionals who can advise and assist you with your marketing plans, especially outreach to the media and community.

The district-level communication/PR office generally acts as a clearinghouse for anything related to the media—news releases, letters to local newspapers, radio or television interviews. Its staff are often looking for "good news" stories to share with the media—not just about teachers and students, but also *your* professional activities and achievements.

In working with communication/PR staff, the same guidelines apply as to other types of collaboration. Because their services are often heavily in demand, it is especially important to:

- Follow the communication policies and guidelines they provide.
- Use the forms provided for a parent or guardian to grant permission for student photos and comments to appear in the news media.
- Build and nurture relationships with key staff.
- Keep them informed of library activities.
- Know what they can and can't do.
- Meet their deadlines.
- Let them know you appreciate their services.

In some districts, school staff are not allowed to create their own promotional materials but are required to use district staff. Providing the professionally designed and ready-to-use @ your library® logo and campaign materials can make their jobs easier.

If your district or school does not have communication expertise, you may wish to recruit a parent or other volunteer with this expertise. Promoting the library might also make for an intriguing class project.

Contributor: Harriet Selverstone, an adjunct visiting professor at Pratt Institute's Graduate School of Information and Library Science. She is a past president of the American Association of School Librarians.

Marketing to All

Libraries are places where students can learn about people who are both similar to and different from themselves. They should also be places where students' differences are acknowledged and respected. In marketing your school library media program, you will want to address a wide range of differences stemming from physical, mental or emotional abilities, language, racial, socioeconomic or cultural background.

Communicating a warm welcome is especially important for children and parents who may have had little experience with libraries. This includes a comfortable physical environment, collections that help students learn about their differences, and staff who are sensitive to these differences. Working to develop projects that celebrate the spectrum of humanity communicates that the media center is central to teaching and learning about diversity in all forms.

Reaching Out to Children with Disabilities

Today there are many new and increasingly affordable assistive technologies that can help to ensure all students become successful seekers and users of information. Susan Gilbert Beck, president of Emanda, Inc. and a consultant on library access, offers the following guidelines.

- Be sensitive in your use of language, both when speaking and in developing signage, publications and other materials. A child is far from being totally described by a disability.
- Assess your media center's traffic patterns and use of space to ensure there is adequate access for wheel chairs.
- Make sure your Web page is friendly to users of various physical and mental abilities. You can gauge its accessibility at *http://bobby.watchfire.com/bobby/html/en/index.jsp.* You also will find guidelines for using screen readers like JAWS, the Kurzweil print reader and other assistive technologies that enhance readability for people with vision difficulties.
- Assess the availability of on-site assistive and adaptive software and equipment and make improvements if necessary.
- Offer awareness training to the library (and school) staff. If communication seems to be a problem, consider what solutions might be reasonable and considerate. Staff should know proper approaches to promoting library programs to children with deafness, blindness, mental illness, learning and other disabilities and helping them to participate.
- Join an electronic discussion list that addresses libraries and disability access. To subscribe, send an e-mail to *listserv@maelstrom.stjohns.edu.* In the body of the message, type: subscribe axslib-l [your first and last name].

For more information, see:

Against Borders Promoting Books for a Multicultural World by Hazel Rochman, ALA Editions, 1993.

Cultural Diversity in Libraries by Donald E. Riggs and Patricia A. Tarin, Neal-Schuman Publishers, 1994

Cultural Diversity and Gender Equity, an extensive curriculum resource list from the Otto-Blair Middle School, Blair, NE. *www.esu3.org/districts/Blair/OBMS/curriculum/social_studies/culture_gender.html.*

Equal Access to Software and Information (EASI), Training on barrier-free Web design and other matters. *www.rit.edu/~easi*

Designing a More Usable World—for All, Trace Research & Development Center, University of Wisconsin, College of Engineering. A guide to products, technologies, training and techniques to eliminate barriers and create expanded opportunities. *www.trace.wisc.edu*

ERIC Clearinghouse on Counseling and Student Services. Highlights articles, resources and research on serving culturally diverse students from elementary through college level. *http://ericcass.uncg.edu/virtuallib/diversity/diversitybook.htmlER*

LD Online, the leading Web site on learning disabilities for parents, teachers and other professionals. *www.ldonline.org*

"Tech for Kids With Disabilities" by Harriet Selverstone, *School Library Journal*, June 2003, p. 36.

U.S. Department of Justice Web site. For information about federal laws and resources, see the page on disabilities at *www.usdoj.gov/disabilities.htm.*

Venture into Cultures, Second Edition, A Resource Book of Multicultural materials and Programs, Olga R. Kuharets, Ethnic and Multicultural Exchange Round Table (EMIERT), ALA Editions, 2001.

Bridging the Culture Gap

In developing your marketing/communication plan, keep in mind these suggestions from Denise Agosto, an instructor in the MLS program at Rutgers, the State University of New Jersey. For more good ideas, see her article "Bridging the Culture Gap: Ten Steps Toward a More Multicultural Youth Library"(*Journal of Youth Services in Libraries*, Spring 2001, 38–41).

- Re-evaluate your mission statement to ensure that it reflects your media center's commitment to serving students of all backgrounds to live in a diverse society.
- Assess your library's physical environment. The artwork, displays and overall décor of your library all provide opportunities to highlight the diversity of cultures represented in your student body and beyond. (ALA Graphics offers posters and other promotional materials representing many cultures.)
- Diversify your collection. Agosto notes that even if money is tight, your collection should reflect a commitment to building a collection that is multicultural in all aspects—racial, linguistic, religious, gender, disability, political, geographic, age and socioeconomic.
- Emphasize collaboration—with other librarians, teachers and community leaders. Agosto calls it being a "Multicultural Ambassador." Working with teachers to develop research projects with multicultural themes promotes learning on many levels.
- Foster dialog. Encourage students to do more than read. Sponsor a bookclub and other opportunities to discuss the people and ideas and issues they read about. Build programming around cultural celebrations such as Latino Heritage Month, Polish Heritage Month and Cinco de Mayo.
- Engage your community. Invite a parent, religious leader and representatives of other culturally diverse groups to speak, perform or help students to learn about different aspects of other cultures such as food or art. Those invited will learn too—about the media center, school and your commitment to all the youth of your community.

To download the new print-ready graphics for school libraries, go to *www.ala.org/@yourlibrary,* click on *School Library Campaign*, and then *Graphics.*

Media Relations

Every school and school district has newspapers, newsletters and other publications directed at students, teachers, administrators and parents. Some have radio or TV stations. You may also want to reach out to community media with announcements of grants or awards or special events such as the grand re-opening of the media center, a Read and Rock-a-thon or visit by a well known author. It helps to generate media interest if the event is held in connection with National Library Week, School Library Media Month or other nationally recognized observance. (See **"Calendar of Promotional Opportunities"** on page 35.)

In reaching out to the media, make sure you know and follow your school district's policies and procedures. You will also want to coordinate media outreach with other media centers in the district so local media is not bombarded with similar press materials. See **"Working with School District Level PR Staff"** on page 17 for more suggestions. For resources on dealing with the media, see the ALA *Online Media Relations Toolkit* compiled by the ALA Public Information Office under **"More Tools"** on page 39.

You will want to develop a contact person at each media outlet. You also will want to check on guidelines, deadlines and whether it is best to mail, fax, or e-mail copy. Many publications and stations post this information on their Web sites. Keep news releases to the point and include a contact name and information. Be sure to mention photo opportunities, especially for television. Some smaller newspapers may accept photos you submit. Producers of radio talk shows often are looking for guest experts to interview on intriguing topics, e.g., "What Every Parent Should Know about the Internet" or "It's Critical to Your Child's Education—and It's not their Teacher."

Use the sample press documents as models for developing your own materials. If your school district has a communication department, send your copy and ask for assistance in reaching out to local media. Remember that even if the release isn't used, it will help to educate the editors and may inspire a story at a later date.

The press documents can be downloaded at *www.ala.org/@yourlibrary.* Click on *School Library Campaign,* then *Media Relations.*

Sample Opinion Column

An opinion column or letter to the editor can help to get your message before the public. Clearly representing the opinion of the writer, these columns generally appear on the "op-ed" (opposite the editorial) page. When writing an op-ed, you will need:

- an attention-getting opening that states the problem;
- your key message and three key points that reinforce it;
- statistics and examples—local/state/national—that illustrate your points;
- a close that summarizes and reinforces your case.

While you may draft the piece, it is often better to have it signed and submitted by a respected figure such as the principal, school board president, parent or other advocate. Other options are letters to the editor, which are more succinct, or editorial endorsements. For example, if your library has undergone a much-needed renovation, you may wish to write a letter-to-the-editor thanking taxpayers for their investment and explaining what it will mean for students. If the library is being unfairly targeted for cuts, you may wish to recruit an advocate to seek an editorial in support of funding for the library media program. Call the editorial page editor or check the Web site for guidelines.

The opinion column on page 21 is intended for a community newspaper or a school district publication for parents or alumni. You will want to read and edit it carefully, adding your own perspective and examples. Or, draft your own column following the above guidelines. Be sure to include a name and contact information, including title, address, daytime telephone number and e-mail. Most newspapers do not want columns longer than 750 words. The sample opinion column in this toolkit is 578 words.

Sample Oped

Support—don't cut—school library media program

One of our most important educational resources is also one of its least valued —the school library media center.

This is unfortunate. When money is tight, tough decisions have to be made, and they are not always good decisions. The pattern in many school districts has been to cut school library media programs first, when they should be last.

A growing body of research confirms that this is a mistake.

Research conducted in eight states shows a direct link between good school libraries and student achievement. These studies, conducted by researcher Keith Curry Lance, Ph.D., of the Library Research Service in Denver, found that students at schools with libraries that are well stocked, well staffed and well-funded consistently score from 10 to 18 percent higher on reading and other tests. This is true whether the schools and their communities are rich or poor, and whether the adults in them are well or poorly educated.

In Williams Intermediate School in Davenport, Iowa, for example, library use increased dramatically during the 2000–01 school year following a revitalization of the library. So did reading scores. Of the 6th graders tested, 18 percent moved from needing improvement to meeting or exceeding reading standards. Test scores for Black and Hispanic students showed even greater gains.

[Add statistics or examples of how your media center makes a difference.]

Think about it. Reading is fundamental to all kinds of learning. Students who read more, read better. Students who can read better, learn better. Students read and learn more if they have a ready supply of quality resources and a knowledgeable guide.

The fact that these truths appear self-evident may explain in part why they have been so often overlooked. There also has been a tendency among many educators—nurtured in part by the technology industry—to believe that putting computers in every classroom is the answer to both learning and spending deficits.

That clearly has not been the case. And the myth that school library media centers would no longer be needed has turned out to be just that—a myth.

Good school library media centers, as defined by Lance, are stocked with a full complement of print and electronic resources and staffed by media specialists with advanced education degrees in teaching and information science. They are a far cry from what most parents remember.

Contrary to what many think, having computers both in the classroom and at home does not mean students have everything they need to learn. Instead, what it often means is that students have developed a false sense that research means doing an Internet search, along with an unhealthy aptitude for plagiarizing thanks to "cut and paste."

In an increasingly complex information environment, knowing how to find information using a variety of sources, how to evaluate it and apply it in an ethical manner is crucial.

School library media specialists teach students the 21st century research skills they will need to learn and achieve in school and throughout their lives. They also work with teaching staff to develop projects and assignments that take students beyond the Web. As wonderful as the Internet is, the vast majority of human knowledge is still contained between two covers.

Savvy educators and parents understand that students need a full range of resources to explore the world of ideas and information. They know there is no such thing as good education without good libraries and that investing in library media programs simply makes good sense. Cutting school libraries is not the answer. Supporting them is.

####

Sample News Release

For release: *[date]*

Contact: *[Name]*
[Telephone]
[E-mail]

Note: *[Highlight photo opportunity here, e.g.: Children will parade through our school dressed as storybook characters on day, date, 2-3 p.m.]*

Celebrating change @ your library

The school library isn't what it used to be. Even its name has changed.

April is School Library Media Month, a time when the American Library Association and American Association of School Librarians remind us about the critical role these learning centers play.

The *[Name of library]* will be celebrating throughout the month with special programs and activities for students, teachers and parents. These include *[list events, dates, times]*.

Far from being "just books," today's school library media center connects students with a wide range of media, including books, videos, CD-ROMs and the Internet—not to mention databases and other online resources most parents don't know how to use.

"Every student succeeds at your library," *[Full name, title, school]* explains. "It's one place where kids aren't expected to know all the answers. That's why we're here—to teach them how to find the answers."

Research shows there is a direct link between student achievement and school library media programs that are staffed by professional media specialists and stocked with a full range of print, electronic and other resources.

Keith Curry Lance, Ph.D., an educational researcher who has conducted studies in eight states, found that students at schools with good libraries consistently scored from 10 to 18 per cent higher on reading and other achievement tests regardless of the economic and educational levels of adults in the community.

[Last name] says *[he/she]* finds *[his/her]* work both important and fun.

"Reading is a joy. I love helping students find just the right book," *[Last name]* explains. "I also love the thrill of the chase, helping students and teachers find the answers they need and teaching them to be information savvy. I feel like I'm making a difference in their lives not just today, but 10 or 20 years from now."

On any given day, students may seek *[his/her]* help in researching immigration from Russia, a cure for SARS or the role of women in the Civil War. *[She/He]* also works with teachers to design projects that challenge students' research skills.

"Finding information today is a whole different ballgame," explains *[Last name]*. "And Google isn't always the best source. Students today must know how to use both print and online resources if they are to succeed in school and throughout their lives. Even teachers don't always know what is out there."

To learn more about what's happening at the *[name of library,]* check out its Web page *[insert web address]* or drop by.

####

Sample Public Service Announcements (PSAs/PA)

Radio and TV stations will often run brief announcements of public interest for free as time permits. Cable stations are more likely to run school-related announcements. Some, in fact, may welcome messages appropriate for airing during school board or other civic/educational broadcast. Check online or contact the community service or public affairs director for time, length and other guidelines. Some television stations will run a slide or video with the announcement. If you have a school or school district radio or TV station that will help produce spots, you're in luck. You may also adapt them for PA announcements. Here is some sample copy to get you started. Be sure to edit appropriately. Recruit student to help in writing and delivering the message in a way that speaks to their peers.

For parents. . .

10 sec   Every student succeeds at the school library. Check out what's new. Visit or log on at *[url]*.

20 sec   Every student succeeds at the school library. Research shows that students who achieve have good school libraries. It's where they learn how to find the answers they need—for a lifetime. To learn more, call or visit your child's school library.

30 sec   April is when we celebrate one of our children's most important learning resources—the school library media center. Research shows that students who achieve have good school libraries. It's where they learn how to find the answers they need—for a lifetime. Every student succeeds at your library. To learn more, call or visit your child's school library.

For students. . .

10 sec.   Got questions? Get the answers you need faster and easier—at your library. We're here to help!

10 sec.   Every student succeeds at your library. Study smarter! Research better! Get answers faster at your library.

20 sec.   Study smart! Get answers fast! Leap tall buildings in a single bound! Well, the library may not turn you into Superman, but it can turn you into a super student. Get the help you need . . . at your library!

20 sec.   You've got the Internet at home and you think you're wired. But unless you're connected to the *[Name of library]* you don't know what you're missing. The *[library]* has resources the Internet will never have. Get REALLY connected—at your library.

30 sec.   Stretch your mind. The *[Name of library]* can connect you to a world of knowledge you didn't even know existed. Everything you want to know about practically anything is at your school library. Even better, there's someone to help you find exactly what you need—the media specialist. Believe it or not, the school library media center is one place where you're NOT expected to know the answers. Our job is to help you find them. Drop by or check us out online.

30 sec.   Ace that research project—show your teacher you know how to do more than Google! Learn how to study smarter. . . research better. . . get answers faster! At your library! Believe it or not, the school library media center is one place where you're NOT expected to know the answers. Give your mind a work out. Let the librarian be your personal trainer. You'll find everything you need to know about practically everything at your library! And not even break a sweat.

Advocacy

Promoting library use is one thing. Asking for money is another. Communications that are focused on winning support for a particular issue, point of view or cause—are considered advocacy. Things you might advocate for include a bigger budget (or to avoid a cut), a new or improved facility, adding information literacy to the curriculum, a piece of legislation or other concern you wish to address.

To be effective, an advocacy campaign requires its own communication plan. But before you begin, it's important to know the rules. As employees of tax-supported agencies, school staff may be subject to restrictions—legal and political—as to what form their advocacy may take. Be sure to find out what policies apply. Also seek the counsel of experienced school advocates.

In most cases, the primary audiences for advocacy efforts will be key decision-makers—school and district administrators, board of education members, state or federal legislators. Secondary audiences might be State Department of Education officials, community leaders, other elected officials (the mayor, city or county commissioners), members of the media and others who wield influence with these groups.

While you can, and must, take a leadership role, the best advocates are those who benefit from your work and are willing to speak on your behalf. A Friends of Library group can be the nucleus of your advocacy network. Parent councils, PTAs, teachers' and other groups offer possibilities for extending its reach.

Personal contact, in the form of presentations, visits or calls—especially from someone a board member/legislator knows and respects—is the most powerful form of advocacy. Elected officials also pay close attention to the media. An editorial endorsement from a key newspaper, radio or television station can carry considerable weight. (See **"Media Relations"** on page 20.) There are many other strategies, including letter and postcard campaigns, and demonstrations—depending on your goal.

But don't wait for a crisis.

Decision-makers are more likely to support you if you are already on their radar screen. Be sure to include strategies for staying in regular contact with them as part of your media center's overall marketing communication plan. (See **"Building a Communication Plan"** on page 15.)

For more resources to help you organize an advocacy campaign, see **"More Tools"** on page 39.

Reaching Out to Decision-makers

- Make sure your advocates understand what is at stake and the strategies being used. Provide a message sheet, answers to both basic and difficult questions, key statistics and stories to help them speak with authority.
- Work your contacts. Are there school staff, parents, friends or neighbors who know or have influence with board members or legislators? Ask them if they would be willing to present your case.
- Start sooner rather than later. Make it a point to get support for school library media programs included in forums for candidates. Provide each candidate with a packet of info about the crucial role of the school library media program.
- Send letters of congratulations to winning candidates and an invitation to visit the media center. Add them to the school library's mailing list.
- Maintain a current list/database of decision-makers, especially those that serve in key positions. Include the committees they serve on, their personal and professional background, issues of special concern, the names of their aides and contact information.
- Stay in touch. Have a VIP mailing list. Send your newsletter, annual report and articles of interest, also invitations to art shows and other library-sponsored events. Elected officials often welcome opportunities to mingle with their constituents.
- Make sure they know about your successes. If a student reaches the state science fair with assistance from the media center, send a special flyer or highlight it on page one of your library newsletter. It can be as simple as "Congratulations to Sarah

Student! Sarah will represent our school at the State Science Fair with her project, which examined . . . We're pleased to note that the media center helped Sarah locate several pieces of key research . . ."

- Get them into the library at least once during the school year. Invite them to be special guests at multicultural, literacy or other events hosted by the library—especially if you know the decision-maker has a special interest in that area. Invite them to lead or participate in a discussion of the freedom to read, copyright and other issues.
- Go to board of education meetings. Make it a point to report on the media center's activities at least quarterly. Check to find out what type of reporting is allowed and prepare accordingly.
- Host a meeting of the board @ your library. Provide refreshments and a tour before the meeting.
- Send a basket of cookies, poster, coffee mug or other token to their office with a note thanking them for their support during School Library Media Month.
- Make it clear that you share the board's commitment to quality education. Work with your principal and superintendent to provide information packets on topics such as the "No Child Left Behind" legislation that may help their decision-making, not just about the library media program, but other aspects as well.
- Visit them. Board members and legislators have many voices competing for their attention. It helps to put a face on the cause. The ALA Washington Office (*www.ala.org/washoff*) and many state library associations sponsor legislative days as an opportunity for librarians and their supporters to meet with legislators.
- Make it easy for them to support you. Keep your visits/presentations brief and to the point. Provide a one-page briefing sheet on issues of concern with a clear statement of the action you are seeking, along with other pertinent information. Be sure to include contact information for additional information.
- Support those who support you. If the board of education is endorsing a particular piece of legislation, send a letter or have your Friends group send a letter to key legislators and forward copies to the board.
- Thank them. In person. In writing—and in public (whenever possible). You may wish to write a letter

to the editor or seek a newspaper editorial recognizing a special effort.

Forms of Address

Although most legislators count emails received on a particular issue, there is no substitute for a thoughtful letter mailed or faxed, depending on the urgency.

Congress

Note: For e-mail addresses, see the legislator's Web site or the ALA Legislative Action Center at *http://congress. nw.dc.us/ala/home.*
The Honorable _____
United States Senate
Washington, D.C. 20510

The Honorable _____
United States House of Representatives
Washington, DC 20515

Dear Senator/Representative _____:

State

Governors and Lieutenant Governors:
The Honorable _____
Office of the Governor (Lt. Governor)
State Capital
City/State/ZIP
Dear Governor_____:

Legislators:
The Honorable _____
Address
Dear Representative/Senator:

Board of Education

Dear President/Chairman:
Address members by their names and include titles such as Dr./Mrs./Ms.

Forming a Friends Group

Athletic teams and bands have their boosters. Why shouldn't your school library have a Friends group?

Many public and academic libraries have discovered the advantages of having a Friends' group to support their programs. These include:

- Help with fundraising via membership dues, book sales, other projects;
- Assistance with special projects and programs;
- Advocating for support of the school library media program.

Forming a Friends group can be a key strategy in raising awareness of the library media program, its contributions and needs by engaging parents, school staff and others in its support. It is also an effective way to nurture a core group of advocates in good times, as well as bad.

Recruiting members will be easier if you have already begun to establish a higher profile for the school library media program. You will also want to get the endorsement of school administrators. In approaching them, it may be helpful to submit a brief one-page proposal outlining how the group would work, its goals, purpose, membership and, most important, the advantages it would offer.

Friends of Libraries USA, a national organization that provides support to local Friends groups, offers the following advice for organizing a Friends of a School Library.

1. Determine the purpose of the group. The goal might be the improvement of the library media program. Objectives might include forming a volunteer group or involvement of parents, children, alumni and faculty.
2. Identify and develop a core of lay leaders. The librarian and administration are resources whose involvement and approval are crucial to success.
3. Acquaint the Friends with the basic philosophy and requirements for an effective media program. Define organizational structure, dues structure.
4. Plan an orientation program/welcome event for new members. Explain school policies and procedures, pertinent state and national standards.
5. Develop a communication plan for a membership recruitment campaign. Identify potential members and strategies for reaching them, e.g. news items in parent and faculty newsletters and presentations to parent groups about how school libraries can make a difference in the education of children.
6. Keep records and periodically evaluate the program.
7. Recognize and thank your Friends and volunteers.
8. Decide if Junior Friends (for students) should be an adjunct program.

For more information, including membership, see the FOLUSA Web site at *www.folusa.org*.

Voices of Experience

The following articles share insights and ideas from school library media specialists who have marketed their libraries successfully.

Developing a Market Strategy

By Terri Snethen and Joe Amos

On the front page of the Metropolitan section of the July 7, 2003, *Kansas City* (MO) *Star* was an article about school librarians fighting cuts in their programs. With many other districts facing the same struggles, it has become clear why school library programs and even individual school libraries must develop a marketing strategy.

At Blue Valley North High School we operate a four-tiered marketing plan. The first tier consists of students and faculty. While it should be obvious why we market to the students, as they are the primary reason for our existence, we market just as hard to the faculty because we believe the faculty will be our "Pied Piper" to the students. Approximately 60 to 70 percent of our marketing is aimed at students and faculty and we try to market to each of those groups evenly.

The second tier consists of the administration, both building and district including the school board. Because administrators are the ones making decisions about staffing and budget we must market our successes and ensure that they understand our vital roles as resource providers and curricular leaders. We aim 20 to 30 percent of our marketing toward our administration.

Our third layer is parents. Parents are valuable partners with the library whether helping to get overdue books returned or encouraging students to use the library's resources at home. We direct about 5 to 10 percent of our marketing at parents.

The final tier consists of community patrons. While community members may not to be able use our collections or only use them on-site, we need their support when bond elections come up, as well as in electing school board members who value library

programs and services. Admittedly, we aim less than 5 percent of our marketing strategies directly at the community-at-large.

Many of the strategies we use with students are quite simple, but since our main goal is to keep them aware of library services, we like simple strategies that are easy to implement and easy for the students to recognize. First, we have prominent locations for new books, fiction and nonfiction and advertise their arrival on our Web site. A monthly display advertises and encourages check out of books on a particular subject (Poetry Month, Women's History Month, etc.).

Our school has daily announcements that are read aloud and displayed on monitors throughout the school. We maintain a consistent presence in the announcements with book talks, book club information and book reviews. We advertise not only newer popular titles but also less circulated titles that are great reads.

This year we added peer tutoring to the library media center. Working with counselors and administrators, upper-class tutors were assigned to the library one hour each day. This type of program requires advertising to study hall teachers, so students in study halls can visit the library for help.

We also have marketing and promotional activities aimed at the faculty. In our "Unfavorite Lesson Plan Day" we advertise that librarians are available all day to work with teachers on lesson plans or units they wish to improve. The librarians work with teachers to write improved lesson plans that may or may not include work in the library. It's important that teachers trust that our goal is to support their efforts, not just promote our own program.

We use e-mails to alert the faculty about articles in professional journals, new books, best practices, or even humorous stories and jokes about teaching. There are two characteristics required of these e-mails. The first is a clear subject heading so teachers know exactly what the e-mail is about. This gives the teachers the power to choose what they read. Second, we keep the messages as brief as possible. When sending out e-mails about recent professional articles, include only title, author, page number and a short overview.

Promotional activities share the library's successes with all groups. We celebrate increases in circulation, improved reading scores, more class visits and walk-in traffic in the library. These promotions include write-ups in newsletters, announcements at faculty meetings and a celebration party, complete with cake at the end of the school year. When sharing these successes, we also share the credit. Promoting a sense of ownership among the faculty and administration increases the likelihood that they will support your program during hard times.

Strategies for marketing to the parents include articles in the school's monthly newsletter and presentations at parent's meetings. We have an article about the library in every parent newsletter; topics have included online database resources, professional activities of the library staff, peer tutoring, book club and others. We have the monthly Parent's Club meeting in our library media center during the day, so parents can see the students using library resources. Ask to be allowed to make a presentation to the parents of incoming freshmen outlining all the services the library can offer their students.

It is often difficult to showcase our resources to the community-at-large. Two ways to get community members into your library are to have community meetings held in the library and to have local art shows, which will draw community members who may not have students in school.

Developing marketing strategies is but one part of a good client-centered library program but one we believe to be essential. The attitude of being there to support the successful efforts of the students, faculty, administration, parents and community must premeditate every decision the library staff makes. Using these strategies in our library, student traffic increased 44 percent and circulation increased 16 percent over last year's figures.

How would your library develop a marketing plan similar to what we have outlined here? First, using your library mission, determine your target groups. Second, determine the strengths of your program and the needs of your target groups. Then, plan activities and promotions

that showcase the particular strengths of your program to meet the needs of the identified groups. In good times as well as bad times, a well-designed marketing strategy is a necessary tool to help all client groups appreciate and support the efforts of library staff.

Terri Snethen and Joe Amos are library media specialists at Blue Valley North High School in Overland, KS. Send email to tsnethen@bv229.k12.ks.us.

Stepping Into the Spotlight

By D. Jackson Maxwell, Ph.D.

An idea central to most reform models, including the "No Child Left Behind" legislation, is the need to create community-school interactions. As media specialists, we can serve as the catalysts for creating these interactions. By stepping into the spotlight and assuming the role of promoters and liaisons between our schools, communities and the media, we can help to project positive images of libraries and schools to our stakeholders—and most importantly, parents and taxpayers.

My school, Hamilton Elementary, is an urban, community-based public school located in Memphis, TN. The school serves 750 students of which 86 percent live below poverty level. Hamilton Elementary entered the reform process four years ago. Surveys conducted for the school redesign found that stakeholders did not feel they were adequately informed of school activities. They were unaware of many programs designed to enhance learning and efforts being made to improve community education. At this point, I took up the challenge of establishing better community-school contacts.

The following are some of the media and forums that I've used to put my school library and school in the spotlight.

Newspapers

Too often all we see are negative articles about schools and students. One reason is that no one is informing the newspaper of the good news. It has been my experience that reporters are seeking positive stories. Send a fax or e-mail to let them know about good events happening at your library. The rewards of getting to know education reporters have been great. Hamilton

Elementary averages 10 articles per year in newspapers. One of my suggestions resulted in an article titled "Cool Covers" that described an undertaking by Reading Club students and community volunteers. The article both promoted a creative program for students and recognized the volunteers who contributed their time and energy.

Television and Radio

Like newspapers, television and radio are on the look out for a good story. Contacts with these reporters have been established through phone calls and press releases. Press releases are short with the name, date, time and purpose of an event with a description of why it is newsworthy. Television and radio stations need at least a week's lead-time. A local radio station (WDIA) recently broadcast that Hamilton Elementary received a $2,000 grant for the expansion of innovative library programming. A number of congratulatory messages were received following these broadcasts. One local reporter is assigned to report only good news. He made several trips to our school last year to cover programs like the *Kids On The Block* puppeteer troupe and even to showcase the library media center. Persistence pays!

Electronic Media

Electronic publications are an excellent way to connect with stakeholders. As technology continues to proliferate, the educational community finds itself telecommunicating more and relying less on traditional interaction. Hamilton Elementary's first Web site was designed to provide an additional link between community and school. The site informs parents of teacher assignments, upcoming events, school calendar, extracurricular activities and other school matters. Several pages are dedicated to the library. The library's pages describe special programs, feature pictures of student accomplishments and list library achievements. Students or teachers also can submit work to an ever-increasing number of online publications such as *Kid Pub* or *Cyberkids.* I have used ERIC Documents to publish research findings.

Newsletters, Journals and Magazines

Many newsletters, including those published by schools, boards of education, state departments of education, colleges and professional associations, welcome contributions. School board and state education newsletters often will include pictures and descriptions of student projects. Submitting articles to academic and professional journals keeps you and your school in the news and promotes networking with colleagues around the country. There are numerous education, child psychology, teaching and technology publications, as well as library trade press that welcome articles on a plethora of topics. These venues provide a global audience with whom to share your school library's successes. For example, the regional journal *Tennessee Education* published an article I wrote on using local resources to bridge the gap between school and community.

Conferences, Meetings and Seminars

Conferences are yet another way to showcase library accomplishments. These events bring together many of the top people in the education business. Meetings and seminars also allow you to meet and interact with parents and community members. Parent Teacher Association (PTA) gatherings are great places to announce new projects and successes and to encourage parental involvement. I have also conducted technology seminars for teachers, students and community members to sharpen their computing skills. Such offerings help to build positive lines of communication and goodwill toward the library and its services.

Honors and Awards

Nominating students, fellow teachers, administrators, community members and other librarians for honors and awards can make a positive impact on others by letting them know they are appreciated. Even if they do not receive the honor, most awarding bodies notify the nominee of their consideration as a candidate—which in itself is an honor. I am very thankful to those who have taken time to nominate me.

Library media specialists are in a unique position. As information providers, we have the resources and the skills to focus attention on the accomplishments of students, teachers and our school library programs. Through working with the various media outlets we also develop powerful allies for our schools. By communicating what is right and good about our libraries and schools, we take a huge step toward creating positive self-images and pride in our educational institutions. By taking the lead in promoting our libraries' and our schools' successes, we also increase our own stature in the eyes of our communities and in the field of education.

Dr. D. Jackson Maxwell is library media specialist at Hamilton Elementary School in Memphis, TN, and an educational consultant for Memphis City Schools. He can be reached at: maxwellj01@ten-nash.ten.k12.tn.us.

Facing Challenges

by Rebecca Frager

Our media center, like others, faces many challenges as it attempts to keep pace with the rapidly expanding information environment.

Woodlawn High School is a place where diversity thrives. Of the nearly 1,900 students, 2 percent are Hispanic; 4 percent Asian; 4 percent Caucasian; and 90 percent Black. One of the major challenges is the high rate of transient students. There is about a 50 percent turnover in the student population each year with an almost equal number of new entrants and withdrawals. Many of the students live in foster care or group home environments.

A challenge unique to the library media center is the neglect that it has suffered since the school was established in 1963. Though the library has a number of computers, they are obsolete and do not serve the needs of our students who require streaming video and other multi-media capabilities. The décor is drab and the lighting poor. Computer stations are dispersed throughout the library, making it difficult to have any effective teaching of technology.

The good news is that exciting things are happening. A lab with 30 new computers is under construction. Rather than 28 computer stations in the main library, we will have 15 stations, situated on five round tables. As we continue to weed —and I mean major weeding—we make room for current and relevant information to fill our shelves.

Despite our challenges, Woodlawn is a place where learning happens. And the library media center is, at least in part, responsible for much of the learning that occurs. The media specialists at Woodlawn are committed to our students. My coworker and I spend a lot of time brainstorming ways to promote our library and to get students interested in the resources available to them.

Some of the ways we promote our library:

- We collaborate daily with teachers because we feel that integrating technology into their lesson plans is essential to our students' learning. We provide instruction in all our computer programs. We also work with teachers to develop "Jeopardy"-style games to help prepare students for exams. Teachers bring their classes to the library on the Friday before the test for a session that combines fun and learning. This has been a big hit with both teachers and students.
- Every year we host a Multicultural Day where students from a variety of backgrounds set up display tables promoting their country of origin. Students bring food and artifacts from their country to share with the rest of the students and staff. I make it a point to always have my digital camera at school because we never know when a "Picture Opportunity" may arise. I took pictures of the fair and featured them in the display case stationed just outside the library.
- Each spring we host a poetry contest to coincide with National Poetry Month in April. Students are invited to submit their original poems and attend a public reading of their poetry where judges (usually teachers and counselors) choose the top three. We award a variety of prizes to the winners.
- We do monthly book displays. Our summer display had beach towels, buckets and shovels, a picnic basket and other summer-related items in order to promote reading over the summer. Whatever books we have on display seem to be the ones the kids pick up and want to check out.
- We have an after-school book club attended mostly by girls. We're still working on the guys.
- We also provide tutoring on the computer after school.
- We provide countless booklists to our students ranging from the Black-eyed Susan nominees, to college bound lists, to ALA best picks, and the students' favorite authors. We also make and

distribute bookmarks with quotations about reading or books, or suggestions for reading. These are popular with students.

- Finally, we have a Karaoke Day twice a year. The first is right before winter break, and the second right before the end of the school year. We inform teachers that they may bring their students to the library for some Karaoke fun, if they feel their students have earned this extra privilege. These events give kids a chance to strut their stuff in a very non-threatening environment. They get to see their peers and teachers sing and have fun. They see their librarian and know her on a more intimate level.

In today's world, the library is more than just a place to check out books. It is a place that reflects the real world, from books, to technology, to game playing to singing karaoke. Some may argue that Karaoke has nothing to do with learning or education. But believe me, it gets students and staff into the library. Our students go away with a positive experience, and they come back for more. Our library is a busy place, during the day, during lunch and after school. We literally have to kick students out when it's time for us to go home. Of course the bottom line is whether they are using the resources available to them—and they definitely are.

We have a very difficult and challenging population at Woodlawn — students whom many have given up on. Our goal is to make the library an inviting place. In order to do that, the library must meet their needs. Sometimes those needs include having a good time in a safe place. We give them the tools to improve their lives, we give them positive encouragement, and we give them a safe place where they can feel good about who they are. If the library can be a place of fun as well as learning, then I think we are doing our jobs.

Rebecca Frager is a school library media specialist at Woodlawn High School in Baltimore County, MD. She can be reached at rfrager@bcps.org.

Addressing Your School Board: Tips You Can Use Now

by Sandy Schuckett

Very often, in the course of "school library life," it becomes necessary to speak before your local school board either to insure funding for your library program, or in the worst-case scenario, to save your job.

Although this may seem daunting to some, in reality it is quite simple! Anyone who stands before classes of kids all day or who provides staff development sessions for their school faculties can be equally effective in front of the school board. Imagine that they are all third graders, and it will be easy!

- **Have your message clearly in mind.** Emphasize three, and no more than five, major points. Use facts and figures for emphasis where needed, and always focus on the benefits to *kids*. You will probably have a very short time in which to speak— usually three minutes, and rambling on doesn't work.
- **Write the presentation out.** Use a large font, and double-space it so you can read it or refer to it easily. Underline or highlight the most important points. Read it aloud in advance, and be sure that it fits within the time allotted. If you read it over several times, it will become very familiar to you, and you can just use the paper as a prompt. But don't veer off the text too much because it will use up your time.
- **Smile and look each board member in the eye.** Reach them on a human level, and make them listen to you! DO NOT bury your nose in your notes—this will make for a very boring presentation. Be sure you are close enough to the microphone to be heard clearly. Don't mumble.
- **Do not use library lingo.** No one will understand it. Speak in very simple, basic terms about how a strong school library program advances student achievement. Quote research briefly, and let them know where they can find more details. If you can bring visuals that will enhance the presentation, do so. Colorful graphs or charts that make facts and figures visual work very well, and you can hold them up (or have a colleague do so—or, even a kid!) while you are quoting the figures.
- **Be passionate!** Passion is contagious, and your passionate presentation will get and keep their attention. If you can add humor–do it! People like to laugh.
- **Recruit someone to speak for you.** It often works better if parents, teachers, other community members, or even kids talk about your library

program and its advantages for students. If you can coach them on the potent points mentioned above, and if they speak on behalf of your library, it doesn't seem so much like you are begging for support. They are voters and constituents, and board members are likely to listen to them.

- **Invite as many colleagues as possible.** It doesn't hurt to have a cheering section, and this will show the board members that many more people have a stake in the issue and feel the same way that you do about it.

Once you have addressed your local school board you will realize that it wasn't so hard after all. You will feel great about yourself, and you will know that your words have had an impact. And it only gets easier.

Sandy Schuckett is a past chair of the AASL Legislation Committee. She is writing a book, You Have the Power: Becoming a Successful Political Advocate for School Libraries, *to be published by Linworth Publishing, Inc. in 2004. She can be reached at aq061@lafn.org.*

Ideas Too Good Not to Share

Keep this idea exchange going. Sign up for the AASLPR discussion list (see "**New Tools and Training**" on page 5) or enter your idea on the campaign database at *www.ala.org/@yourlibrary* under *Participating Libraries.*

Outreach to Students

Our school athletes do not always feel comfortable in our library. To encourage them to come in and see that we support them, we have school sport days. This year we had Badminton Day and Track Day. We heavily promoted these events with announcements and displays that featured our holdings on the subject and a schedule of upcoming meets and matches. On the given days, team members came to the library to show off their skills during the last 10 minutes of each lunch period when we're crowded with students. On Badminton Day, we taped off a large square of the room and two of our moveable bin displays served as nets. Other students were allowed to participate, but at least one member of the team had to be "on the floor" at all times. Students quickly saw how much more skill our team members had. On Track Day, we taped a large track around the perimeter of the library and let our track stars jog the track. They lasted longer than our

average student. The coach was quoted as saying, "Thank you for having the Track and Fitness Day, a very good idea to focus attention on the Library Media Center and what can be done to promote school activities."

Sue Gibbs, Gayl Smith and Debbie Turner, Waubonsie Valley High School, Aurora, IL; gayl_smith@ipsd.org.

Outreach to School Boards

None of my 2nd grade students were familiar with the idea of a School Board. After giving them a much-simplified explanation, I had an idea. To celebrate National Library Week, I invited the members of our local school board to be guest readers in the library. Seven of our nine members came in and read to a class from grades K-2. The superintendent of schools and the business manager for the district also read. The students and I thanked each and every one of them for their support of our district's libraries. It was a great experience for all—and it gave me the opportunity to speak with the school board members personally and for them to see the program they fund. During Children's Book Week and National Library Week, I invite different groups of people to be guest readers—grandparents, parents, civic leaders, high school age children of our faculty and staff, husbands of teachers, senior citizens. All of our guest readers receive a thank-you note and photos that I take while they are reading and a posed photograph with the class they have read to. These photos are proudly displayed in our hallway and in many local businesses and offices. This program is so popular I have people asking me if they can read.

Lynn Uhl, Brockway Area School District, Brockway, PA; theuls@key-net.net

Outreach to Parents and Seniors

I've run two programs that were a success with parents and with senior citizens. The first was an evening of interviews with senior citizens about what their lives were like as youngsters in Oneida, especially going to the store and other activities. High school seniors studying economics conducted the interviews and word-processed the responses. The interviews and some pictures of the times were posted on our Web pages. The second program consisted of two evenings of instruction on the Internet along with safety tips and sites to use at home for parents. It was a hands-on workshop. Both programs had excellent administrative support and wonderful media coverage. Senior citizens showed up at the local public library with pals in tow to see "their" Web pages.

Kate Cronn, Oneida Senior High School Library, Oneida, NY; kcronn@oneida-high.moric.org

Celebrating Diversity

I started our Digital Cultural Collage to help students gain an appreciation for the uniqueness of different peoples throughout the world and within our own community. The Digital Cultural Collage consists of videotaped interviews with students of various backgrounds, their photographs and drawings. These are posted on our Web site. I got this idea because I would often converse with our school social worker about how our ESL students were left out during major holiday celebrations. Also, most of our student population has a very limited understanding of what other cultures are like. The idea for the site was developed with our social worker and the ESL teacher. We received a $750 award (not to mention the publicity). We promote the collage by setting aside time during computer/library period to encourage students to explore our library links. Our ESL students are so very proud when they see/hear themselves on the Internet. So far all the ESL students' families have Internet access at home and love the site. I also send an email to my principal and superintendent each time I update the site and put a short article in the district newsletter to call attention to this new library Web page.

Lynn Spencer, Cherry Road School, Syracuse, NY; spencerl@twcny.rr.com

We held a fall multicultural celebration after school to commemorate Hispanic Heritage Month, Native American Heritage Month, Thanksgiving and general December celebrations. Our brand new school Mariachi band, organized by a teacher who loves Hispanic music, played several songs. It was their first public performance. I was surprised and delighted that even some of the musicians' parents came. The teacher herself brought background tapes and taught us several songs, which we sang along with her. A Muslim student who observes Ramadan explained its meaning and how his family observes it. I brought a Menorah, explained about Chanukah and gave everyone chocolate gelt. We also had snacks and drinks. We had great fun and hope to expand the program next year.

Ellie Goldstein-Erickson, Berkeley High School Library, Berkeley, CA; ellie@berkeley.k12.ca.us

Fundraising

At our elementary school we have a birthday book program—families may donate money on behalf of their child for a birthday book. They tell me the child's interests, I try to find a suitable book, read it to the class, then give it to the child as the first person to sign it out. The book has a template that says it has been purchased in recognition of the child's birthday and the date. The response has been terrific. Out of a school population of just over 300, approximately 100 families participated with an average donation of $20. We have raised over $2,100. The kids love it. They especially love having the book read aloud to the class, being the first child to take it out and seeing their name in the book. Often when taking out a book they will look in the front cover to see if it is anyone's birthday book. Younger kids also love it when older students select and read a birthday book to their class. The books have ranged from picture books to adult novels, to art books and fact books, to *Bart Simpson's Guide to Life.*

Kathleen Thomas, Southpointe Academy, Tsawwassen, British Columbia; WTSGREG@aol.com

We had our first Great Summer Reading Sale in May. We began by requesting donations from students and teachers two months before the sale. We placed posters at school and put an article in the school newsletter, which goes home to parents. We decorated a showcase outside the library with information and samples of books that we would be selling. We gave "Free to Read" bookmarks to all who donated and supplemented donations with a small purchase from Goodwill. We accepted paperbacks, hard covers and magazines. We sold paperbacks for 25 cents, hard covers for 50 cents, and gave a free magazine with any purchase. We also raffled off books we had earned from our Scholastic Book Fair and from Books Are Fun. We had books for both students and staff. We sold approximately 600 books and earned $190, which will be used to buy multiple copies of paperbacks for classroom use. Everyone had fun shopping at the bargain prices and there were many requests that we do it again next year. We plan to start taking donations in September.

Janice M. Lauer, Fred Fifer III Middle School, Camden, DE; (302) 698-8400; janice.lauer@caesarrodney.k12.di.us

Promoting Reading

I took pictures with a digital camera of faculty/students reading a favorite book, captioned them, added the @ your library logo, printed and laminated them on color stock. We hung them on the walls of the library's entrance lobby where they got a lot of attention, particularly from students looking at their teachers' selections (which ranged from Philip Roth to Dr. Seuss and everything in between). We had a lot of fun with it. Our head of school is behind a pile of papers, with only the top of her head shown with her hand clutching her hair—her choice is *Alexander and the Terrible, No Good Day*. This is a high school.

Reed Williams, Librarian, Shady Side Academy, Senior School, Pittsburgh, PA; rwilliams@shadysideacademy.org

A very popular idea that both students and adults in this middle/upper school enjoy is a contest to identify the first line of a novel. The line is printed in the daily announcement sheet and the first 10 students to correctly identify the source receive a coupon for rental of a video or DVD from a local store. The Hollywood Video stores provide the coupons free through a program run from their offices at Hollywood

Entertainment (9275 S.W. Peyton Lane, Wilsonville, OR 97070). Faculty report that the students enjoy discussing of the line each day in their morning check-in groups. The students are happy to receive the coupon, especially right before summer vacation begins. Our library serves grades 6-12. The first lines I used were from the first Harry Potter book, *Charlotte's Web*, *Catcher in the Rye*, *Redwall*, *The Great Gatsby*, and *The Adventures of Huckleberry Finn*.

Marghe Tabar, St. Paul Academy & Summit School, St. Paul, MN; mtabar@randolph.spa.edu

"Poetry on Parade" is a schoolwide event celebrated in April during National Poetry Month. "Poetry on Parade" is a program where children learn poetry and then take their poetry "on parade," performing it for other classrooms. Each grade level has a different theme, either a subject like oceans, or a particular poet or genre like Shel Silverstein or haiku. Students make props during art class that relate to their poems. They carry their props when they go on parade. And because classes take turns parading and performing, they also invite other classes to perform in their classroom. There is definitely poetry in the air during the four weeks of the program, culminating in the parade week when parents are invited.

Jane Tretler, Woodland Elementary School, East Syracuse, NY, jtretler@mail.esmschools.org

For more good ideas like these, visit the campaign database: *www.ala.org/@yourlibrary,* and click on *Participating Libraries.*

Calendar of Promotional Opportunities

Taking advantage of special observances to plan school-wide promotions is one way to put your library in the spotlight. If you're clever, you might end up on the 6 o'clock news. Some events, like National Library Week or School Library Media Month are the equivalent of our national holidays. There are many other literacy and literary events that are naturals for libraries, plus thousands more that lend themselves to showing how library media programs support learning on almost any topic . . . everything from Chemistry Month to Be Kind to Pets Week. Many of these observances come "ready made" with publicity materials and ideas for activities.

February

Library Lovers Month

This is a time for everyone, especially Friends of the Library and other library fans, to express their feelings. There is a lively list of activities for libraries and their lovers, including visits from costumed book characters and fundraising ideas. Online postcards and downloadable art for bookmarks, banners and buttons also are provided at *www.librarysupport.net/librarylovers.*

Job Shadow Day, February 2

National Job Shadow Day is a nationwide effort to introduce young people to the world of work by giving them an up-close look at the workplace and to answer questions like "Why do I have to learn this?" or "Why would I want to do this?" AASL and other ALA divisions have endorsed this national initiative as an opportunity to recruit future librarians. A *Job Shadow Day Planning Notebook* and other information can be found at *www.ala.org/aasl/jobshadow.html.*

March

Read Across America, March 2

Started in 1998 as a way to get kids excited about reading, the National Education Association's Read Across America has become the nation's largest reading event. The year-round program culminates each year on or near Dr. Seuss's birthday. Promotion ideas and a "Cat-alog!" of Seussian paraphernalia can be found at *www.nea.org/readacross.*

Freedom of Information Day, March 16

This annual event is observed on or near the birthday of James Madison, the "Father of the Constitution" and the foremost advocate for openness in government. To send online postcards to your favorite teachers and administrators, go to *www2.postcards.org/go/c/0318.* Also see the ALA Washington Office's Web site at *www.ala.org/washoff.* In the left navigation bar, click on *Events* under *Washington Office.*

April

National Poetry Month

Launched in 1996, National Poetry Month brings together libraries, schools, literary organizations and others to celebrate the role of poetry in American culture with readings, festivals, book displays, workshops and other events. The Academy of American Poets sponsors the event. For more information, see *www.poets.org/npm/index.cfm.*

National Volunteer Week

The purpose of this week is to recognize and celebrate the efforts of volunteers at the local, state and national levels. The Volunteer Centers National Network and Points of Light Foundation are sponsors. If you have volunteer helpers and supporters, there's no better time to salute them for what they do. National Volunteer Week will be celebrated April 18–24, 2004

School Library Media Month

School libraries celebrate the month of April as School Library Media Month. Sponsored by AASL, it has the same theme as National Library Week. For tips and suggested activities, see *www.ala.org/aasl/slmmonth.html.*

National Library Week

First sponsored in 1958, National Library Week is a national observance sponsored by the American Library

Association (ALA) and libraries across the country each April. It is a time to celebrate the contributions of our nation's libraries and librarians and to promote library use and support. Tips for organizing and promoting are posted on The Campaign for America's Libraries Web site at *www.ala.org/@yourlibrary*. Click on *PR Tools and Resources*. NLW will be held April 18–24, 2004.

Young People's Poetry Week

Celebrated the third week in April, this annual event is sponsored by the Children's Book Council (CBC), to highlight poetry for children and young adults and encourage everyone to celebrate poetry—read it, enjoy it, write it. A downloadable poster and other support materials are available at *www.cbcbooks.org/html/poetry_week.html*

TV Turn-off Week

The week is sponsored each April by the TV Turn-off Network, whose motto is "Turn off TV. Turn on Life." Why not send a flyer with TV free activity ideas home with students? For more ideas, see *www.tvturnoff.org*. TV Turn-off Week is April 19–25, 2004.

World Book and Copyright Day, April 23

An ideal opportunity to talk about copyright, plagiarism and other issues related to intellectual property. Sponsored internationally by UNESCO,this day is a symbolic one for world literature. On this date and in the same year of 1616, Cervantes, Shakespeare and Inca Garcilaso de la Vega died. It is also the date of birth or death of several other prominent authors. See *www.unesco.org/culture/bookday*.

El día de los niños/El día de los libros, April 30

This annual celebration of children, families and reading focuses on the importance of advocating literacy for every child regardless of linguistic and cultural background. It is sponsored by the Association for Library Service to Children (ALSC) with the National Association to Promote Library and Information Services to Latinos and the Spanish Speaking (REFORMA). Go to *www.ala.org/alsc*. Look under *Projects and Partnerships*.

May

Get Caught Reading Month

This nationwide campaign aims to remind people of all ages how much fun it is to read. The observance is sponsored by the Association of American Publishers (AAP) and the Magazine Publishers of America (MPA). Check out the suggestions for activities and support materials at *www.getcaughtreading.com*.

National PTA Teacher Appreciation Week

Sponsored since 1984, the week offers an opportunity to let teachers know how much you appreciate their hard work. Learn more at *www.pta.org*. This week is being celebrated May 2–8, 2004.

National Library Legislative Day

National Library Legislative Day, cosponsored by the District of Columbia Library Association and the American Library Association, is held each year in May to bring librarians, library trustees, board members and other library friends to Washington, D.C., to talk with their representatives and senators about issues of concern. This includes funding for school libraries. Be there if you can. For information, visit the ALA Washington Office's site at *www.ala.org/washoff*. In the left navigation bar, click on *Events* under *Washington Office*.

September

Library Card Sign-Up Month

A time when the American Library Association and libraries across the country remind parents that the most important school supply of all is @ your library®—it's your library card. Thousands of public and school libraries join together each fall in this national effort. Posters and other promotional materials are available from ALA Graphics. For good ideas on how to organize, go to *www.ala.org/pio*. Click on *Promotions* and then *Library Card Sign-Up Month*.

International Literacy Day, September 8

A time to ask: What would your life be like if you couldn't read? This annual event, sponsored by the

International Reading Association and United Nations Educational, Scientific and Cultural Organization (UNESCO) is an opportunity to focus on the 875 million adults worldwide who do not know how to read or write. Nearly two-thirds are women. For info, see *www.reading.org/meetings/ild.*

Banned Books Week: Celebrating the Freedom to Read

Observed during the last week of September each year, this annual event is an opportunity to educate about one of our most precious freedoms in a democracy and the role of libraries. A Banned Books Week Kit, list of "The 100 Most Challenged Books" and other materials are available from the ALA Office for Intellectual Freedom at *www.ala.org/oif.*

October

Computer Learning Month

This annual event focuses on the important role that computers, software and other technologies play in our lives, particularly in children's learning and their future. The Computer Learning Foundation provides activities, generally in the form of merit competitions and sweepstakes, to encourage people to explore new ways of using technology and to share their knowledge with others in their community. For more information, see *www.computerlearning.org/clmact.htm.*

International School Library Day

Observed the third Monday in October, this day is sponsored by the International Association of School Librarianship to focus on the richness and variety of school library services in different countries, and the contribution that they make to their schools and communities. For activity and publicity ideas, see *www.iasl-slo.org/schoollibraryday.html.*

National Book Month

This annual celebration of writers and readers is sponsored by the National Book Foundation. Finalists for the prestigious National Book Awards for U.S. authors, including Young People's Literature, are announced in October. The awards presentation is in November. Take advantage of this opportunity to engage students in discussing the nominees and what makes a winning book in their eyes, as well as the judges'. For ideas on how to celebrate, see *www.nationalbook.org/nbm.html.*

National Storytelling Festival

The International Storytelling Center celebrates the power of storytelling each year in October by showcasing the world's stories, storytellers and storytelling traditions at the National Storytelling Festival—the world's premier storytelling event—in Jonesborough, TN. Why not hold your own festival and get students and teachers involved in this ancient and fun tradition? Learn more at *www.storytellingcenter.com/festival/festival.htm.*

Teen Read Week

Observed the third week of October, this annual celebration is sponsored by ALA and its Young Adult Services Association to encourage teens to "read for the fun of it." The ALA Graphics Catalog offers a wealth of promotional materials. Ideas for celebrating and sample publicity materials are provided online. Go to *www.ala.org/yalsa* and click on *Teen Read Week.*

November

American Education Week

Sponsored by the National Education Association, this annual event celebrates the educators and school staff who keep children safe, healthy, and help them achieve. That includes you! The 2003 observance is November 16–22, 2003. Tools, including downloadable artwork, are provided at *www.nea.org/aew.*

Children's Book Week

Observed since 1919, Children's Book Week encourages children and the adults who care for them to spend some time with a book each day. Children's Book Week 2003 is November 17-23. Tips for organizing and publicizing, including a downloadable poster, are available from the Children's Book Council at *www.cbcbooks.org/html/book_week.html.*

Family Literacy Day, November 1

Sponsored by the National Center for Family Literacy, this annual event celebrates the important role of parents in their children's learning. "Useful Tools," including planning celebration tips, publicity materials and a calendar of parent-child activities, are provided at www.famlit.org.

For more good ideas, see:

Chase's Calendar, a compendium of holidays, celebrations and other observances around the world. Published annually by McGraw-Hill Professional.

The Teacher's Calendar: The Day-by-Day Directory to Holidays, Historic Events, Birthdays, and Special Days, Weeks, and Months by Sandy Whiteley (Compiler). Published annually by McGraw-Hill

Get the score

@ your library®

Whether you're researching current events, sports statistics or facts for that term paper, we have the information you're looking for.

The Campaign for America's Libraries

To download the new print-ready graphics for school libraries, go to www.ala.org/ @yourlibrary, click on *School Library Campaign*, and then *Graphics*.

More Tools

For more helpful tools and information about marketing, programming and promotion, see these resources available from ALA and AASL.

Advocacy

AASL Advocacy Toolkit: *www.ala.org/aasl/advocacy*
A collection of ready-to-use tools to conduct an advocacy campaign—large or small—for school library media programs, including quotable facts about school library media centers, "What Parents Should Know" and a wealth of other resources.

AASL Introduction to Advocacy and Advocacy Training:
www.ala.org/aasl/advocacy/aasl_adv_train_web0502.ppt
This PowerPoint presentation provides a basic framework for launching an advocacy effort on behalf of your school library media program.

ALA Resolution: School Libraries and Librarians are Critical to Educational Success:
www.ala.org/aasl/advocacy/resolution.html
At its June 2003 meeting, the Council of the American Library Association unanimously passed this resolution in support of school libraries and librarians.

ALAWON
A free, irregular publication of the ALA Washington Office provides updates and alerts on federal legislation, including funding for school library media centers. To subscribe, send an e-mail message to *listproc@ala1.ala. org*. Leave the subject line blank. In the body of the message, type: subscribe ala-wo [your first and last name].

Information Power **Basic Implementation Kit:**
www.ala.org/aasl/ip_basic.html
This PowerPoint presentation is designed for use by building-level school library media specialists to introduce the standards and principles of *Information Power: Building Partnerships for Learning* to an audience of parents, teachers and/or building administrators.

Information Power: Building Partnerships for Learning
Brochure: *www.ala.org/aasl/ip_brochure.html*

A great tool to use with your educational partners when advocating for Information Power in your school or district. The brochure lists the Nine Information Literacy Standards and suggests ways that Information Power can benefit students, teachers, library media specialists and administrators. Available in packs of 25 for $8/pack (plus shipping and handling). To order call 866-SHOP ALA (866-746-7252).

Library Advocacy Now!: *www.ala.org.* Click on *Issues and Advocacy* from the ALA homepage. Resources for library advocates from the American Library Association, including the *Library Advocate's Handbook* and other downloadable support materials.

Principal's Manual Brochure:
www.ala.org/aasl/principalsmanual.html
This brochure is designed to guide the principal in assessing and planning for the school library media program. Offered as an aid to principals as they prepare with school library media staff, district administrators, teachers, students and parents for the next school year. The brochure is available online in PDF format (*www.ala.org/aasl*) and in packs of 25 for $8/pack (plus shipping and handling). To order call 866-SHOP ALA (866-746-7252). Request a free single copy by sending a self-addressed stamped envelop (no smaller than a no. 10 size) to AASL Principal's Manual Brochure, 50 E. Huron St., Chicago, IL 60611-2795.

For additional resources, see the "Public Relations" bibliography (www.ala.org/aasl/resources/pr.html), part of the AASL Resource Guides for School Library Media Program Development.

Graphics

@ your library logos: *www.ala.org/@yourlibrary*
Click on *Download Logos*.
The @ your library logo is available for downloading in color and black and white in a variety of publishing programs for MAC and PC formats.

ALA Online Store: *www.alastore.ala.org*
ALA Graphics is the official sponsor of @ your library products promoting libraries and literacy. Posters,

bookmarks, coffee mugs, t-shirts, pins and more are available. Also see the *ALA Graphics Catalog.* To order, call 800-545-2433, press 7.

Media Relations

ALA Online Media Relations Toolkit: *www.ala.org/pio*
Click on *Online Member Media Relations Tools.*
The ALA Public Information Office has compiled a list of resources to help you prepare and discuss key library messages and hot topics such as Information Literacy, CIPA and Better Salaries. Also links to media relations strategies, crisis communications plans, library advocacy materials and more.

National Campaigns and Promotions

Campaign for America's Libraries:
www.ala.org/@yourlibrary
The Campaign for America's Libraries is a multi-year public education effort sponsored by the American Library Association to speak loudly and clearly about the value of libraries and librarians in the 21st century. You'll find programming ideas, sample press materials, downloadable logos and photos, print-ready artwork, video links, advocacy resources, suggestions for National Library Week, School Library Media Month, and more.

ALA Promotional Events: *www.ala.org.* Click on *Events and Conferences.* On the left hand side of the screen, click on *Library Promotions.*
Links to National Library Week, School Library Media Month, Banned Books Week, LIVE @ your library and other national initiatives from the American Library Association that provide great opportunities for marketing and promotion.

Scholastic Library/Grolier National Library Week Grant: An annual $5000 award given to any U.S. library that prepares the best proposal for a National Library Week promotion tied to the @ your library brand. Application typically posted in early August. Deadline: mid-October. Winning library notified in early January and announced at ALA Midwinter Meeting. Sponsored by Scholastic Library Publishing and administered by the ALA Public Awareness Committee. For an application, go to *www.ala.org/@yourlibrary.*

Organizations

ALA Public Information Office: *www.ala.org/pio*
The ALA Public Information Office develops and implements strategic communications plans tied to association goals and priorities in the areas of media relations, advocacy, public education and crisis communications. The department also provides public relations counsel and media training and support to ALA executive staff, officers and members; coordinates national media relations efforts; organizes an advocacy network; develops public relations support materials for libraries; and is responsible for the implementation of @ your library®, The Campaign for America's Libraries.

American Association of School Librarians:
www.ala.org/aasl
The American Association of School Librarians (AASL) is a professional membership organization, serving the needs of 10,000 school library media specialists in the United States, Canada and around the world. Its mission is to advocate excellence, facilitate change, and develop leaders in the school library media field. AASL promotes the improvement and extension of library media services in elementary and secondary schools as a means of strengthening the total education program.

ALA Washington Office: *www.ala.org/washoff*
This office includes the Office of Government Relations, which acts as a link between ALA members and the federal government on issues relating to the quality of library and information services available to the American public, and the Office for Information Technology Policy (OITP), which promotes the development and use of electronic access to information as a means to ensure the public's right to a free and open information society. The Washington Office hosts a federal Legislative Day each May. To learn more, go to *www.ala.org.* Look under *Our Association* for *Offices.*

Publications

Information Power: Building Partnerships for Learning, AASL/AECT
Includes the *Information Literacy Standards for Student Learning* that will help students become skillful producers and consumers of information along with the guidelines and principles that will help you create a dynamic, student-centered program. Available from the ALA

Online Store at *http://alastore.ala.org* or call 866-SHOP ALA (866-746-7252).

Ideas for Promoting Your School Library Media Program, Ann Wasman, ed.

An expansion of AASL's original *On Target,* this publication takes program promotion beyond School Library Media Month with advice and suggestions for year-round promotion. It answers questions on how to get started and presents ideas for various school library media activities and programs, from cooperative efforts to electronically-inspired activities. Information about other sources and materials helpful in promotional efforts is included. To order call 866-SHOP ALA (866-746-7252).

The Information-Powered School, Sandra Hughes-Hassell and Anne Wheelock, eds.

Contains more than 40 templates and model forms, all tested in actual Library Power sites. Outlines a specific plan for how school library media specialists and teachers can work in collaboration. Includes tips from experienced practitioners on gathering the support of teachers and principals. See chapter 10, "Community Engagement for Information Power." Available from the ALA Online Store at *http://alastore.ala.org* or call 866-SHOP ALA (866-746-7252).

Library Advocate's Handbook: *www.ala.org.* Click on *Issues and Advocacy, Resources,* and then *Advocacy Publications.*

Tips for developing a library advocacy plan and network @ your library. Includes communication planning strategies, how to generate key messages and prepare spokespeople. Includes a checklist of advocacy activities. Print copies $5 from the ALA Public Information Office. Free when distributed as part of ALA's Library Advocacy Now! Training. Call 800-545-2433, ext 5044 to order. Email: *advocacy@ala.org*

MLS Marketing Library Services:
www.infotoday.com/mls/mls.htm
Bi-monthly newsletter from Information Today, Inc., that provides information professionals in all types of libraries with specific ideas for marketing their services, including suggestions for planning programs, making money, increasing business and proving your value to your administrators.

New Steps to Service: Common-Sense Advice for the School Library Media Specialist, Ann M. Wasman
Recent library media school graduates, non-librarians and others unfamiliar with the process may find setting up and running a school library media center a daunting task. New Steps to Service is a user-friendly, practical guide for creating and maintaining a school library media center that works for students and you. Available from the ALA Online Store at *http://alastore.ala.org* or call 866-SHOP ALA (866-746-7252).

Power Tools: 100+ Essential Forms and Presentations for Your School Library Media Program, Joyce Kasman Valenza
A toolkit that includes a booklet, CD-ROM, copy-ready forms, and four slide shows. Topics include public relations, day-to-day stuff, information skills, graphic organizers and the Internet. Appendices include recommended resources and library related quotes. Although out of print, a revised edition—*Power Tools Recharged*—will be published by ALA Editions in June 2004.

Shy Librarian: Promoting Libraries, Librarians and Books
www.shylibrarian.com
THE SHY LIBRARIAN is a quarterly, ad-free, print magazine, which focuses on "promoting libraries, librarians and books," with many articles on library marketing, public relations and programming. Also featured are over 50 original reviews of new books for children and young adults, as well as reviews of professional books written by librarians and teachers.

Recruitment

School Librarianship as a Career: *www.ala.org/aasl/career*
Developed by the AASL Recruitment for the Profession Committee, this Web site is a collection of resources and information about becoming a school library media specialist.

Research

Capitalizing on the School Library's Potential to Positively Affect Student Achievement: A Sampling of Resources for Administrators:
www.unocoe.unomaha.edu/ghartzell/library
Dr. Gary Hartzell's White House conference presentation that includes a bibliography of 50 years' worth of studies showing school library impact, materials on the role of the principal in quality library media programs and

persuasion materials (links to PowerPoint presentations and other items).

How School Librarians Help Kids Achieve Standards:
www.lrs.org/documents/lmcstudies/CO/execsumm.pdf
Executive summary of the second "Colorado Study" conducted by Keith Curry Lance, Marcia J. Rodney and Christine Hamilton-Pennell.

For additional resources, see the "Student Achievement" bibliography (www.ala.org/aasl/resources/achievement.html), part of the AASL Resource Guides for School Library Media Program Development.

Library Impact Studies:
www.lrs.org/Impact_study.htm#AK
Results of studies conducted by the Library Research Service, based in Denver, on the impact of school library media centers in eight states: Alaska, Iowa, Maryland, Minnesota, North Carolina, Oregon, Pennsylvania and Texas.

School Library Campaign Research:
www.ala.org/@yourlibrary
Click on *School Library Campaign* and then *Research*. Washington, DC-based KRC Research conducted a series of interviews and focus groups within the school library community, as well as with students, teachers, parents and principals in Baltimore, Indianapolis and Phoenix to determine the best way to communicate about the value of school libraries and librarians in the 21st century. Key messages and talking points were developed by KRC, based on that research and further discussion with AASL members.

State Campaigns and Promotions

"Building Skills for Tomorrow: Minnesota School Library Media Programs Make a Difference":
www.isd77.k12.mn.us/memo/memo.html
Promotional video created by the Minnesota Educational Media Organization (MEMO), an affiliated organization of the American Association of School Librarians. The video can be downloaded in QuickTime format. Links to the script and handouts for principals and parents for the video are included.

"The Very Best Place to Start": *http://statelibrary.dcr.state. nc.us/ld/youth/ysap/very_best.htm*
The State Library of North Carolina's awareness campaign includes public service announcements and campaign tools and templates.

Open a book, open your mind

At your school library media center, books are just the beginning.

@ your library®

The Campaign for America's Libraries

To download the new print-ready graphics for school libraries, go to *www.ala.org/@yourlibrary,* click on *School Library Campaign,* and then *Graphics.*

School Library Campaign Feedback Form

Please help us gauge the success of our efforts for this @ your library® initiative by completing this evaluation form and faxing it to AASL at 312-664-7459. An online form also is available at *www.ala.org/yourlibrary.* Click on *School Library Campaign.*

1. How did you learn about/acquire your @ your library® toolkit?
   ❑ Journal/other publication
   ❑ ALA/AASL Web site
   ❑ AASL National Conference
   ❑ Other (please specify): _____

2. What aspects of the toolkit/Web site did you find most helpful? (Please check all that apply):
   ❑ Ideas and suggestions
   ❑ Messages and slogans
   ❑ Sample publicity materials
   ❑ Outreach strategies
   ❑ Downloadable graphics
   ❑ Communication plan guide
   ❑ More tools

3. What do you think of the campaign's key messages? Are there any talking points you would add or delete?

   _____
   _____
   _____
   _____
   _____

4. How are you participating in the campaign and using the @ your library® brand (i.e., marketing efforts, promotional materials, programming, special events, etc.)? Please provide a brief description.

   _____
   _____
   _____
   _____
   _____

5. If you have used any of the sample press materials, have you received any media coverage? Please describe.

   _____
   _____
   _____
   _____
   _____

6. Are there additional tools and materials that you would like ALA and AASL to provide? Please be specific.

   _____
   _____
   _____
   _____
   _____

Other comments:

   _____
   _____
   _____
   _____
   _____
   _____
   _____

The *@ your library® Toolkit for School Library Media Programs* is published by the American Library Association (ALA) and the American Association of School Librarians (AASL), a division of ALA.

Editor

Linda Wallace

Special contributors

Joe Amos
M. Veanna Baxter
Susan Gilbert Beck
Rebecca Frager
Friends of Libraries USA
D. Jackson Maxwell, Ph.D.
Sandy Schuckett
Harriet Selverstone
Terri Snethen

Acknowledgements

ALA and AASL wish to thank 3M Library Systems for their generous and continuing support of The Campaign for America's Libraries and to our members for sharing their time and insights.

School Library Campaign Special Committee

Chair

Harriet S. Selverstone
Adjunct Visiting Professor
Pratt Institute
Graduate School of Information and Library Science
Library Media Consultant
Westport, CT

Members

Sandra Kennedy Bright
Director, School Library Services
New York City Board of Education
Brooklyn, NY

Connie Champlin
Media Tech Consulting
Indianapolis, IN

Keith Curry Lance, Director
Library Research Service
Denver, CO

Jeanne Martinez, Component Director
Education Service Center, Region 20
San Antonio, TX

Judi Lynn Moreillon
Library Media Specialist
Sabino High School
Tucson, AZ

Frances R. Roscello
Associate in School Library Media Services
Office of New York City School and Community Services
New York State Education Department
Albany, NY
President, AASL (2003–04)

J. Linda Williams, Director
Library Media Services
Anne Arundel County Public Schools
Crofton, MD

Julie A. Walker, Executive Director
American Association of School Librarians
Ex-Officio

Toolkit Group

Harriet S. Selverstone
Frances R. Roscello

M. Veanna Baxter
Adjunct Professor
Mansfield University
Library Science and Information Technologies
Principal, VBEC Library Consulting Services
New Holland, PA

Terry Young
Library Media Specialist
West Jefferson High School
New Orleans, LA

ALA Staff

Deborah Davis (PIO)
Megan Humphrey (PIO)
Steven Hofmann (AASL)
Jennifer Locke (AASL)
Andrea Parker (AASL)

Contacts

Campaign for America's Libraries
ALA Public Information Office
Tel: 800-545-2433, ext. 2148/4020
E-mail: *atyourlibrary@ala.org*

American Association of School Librarians
Tel: 800-545-2433, ext. 1396
E-mail: *aasl@ala.org*